DATE DUE

THE SECOND EPISTLE OF SAINT PAUL
TO THE CORINTHIANS

THE SECOND EPISTLE
OF SAINT PAUL
TO THE CORINTHIANS

JEAN HÉRING

1 3 7 1 9

*Professor Emeritus in the Faculty of Protestant Theology
in the University of Strasbourg*

Translated from the First French Edition by
A. W. Heathcote and P. J. Allcock

LONDON
THE EPWORTH PRESS

FIRST PUBLISHED BY
DELACHAUX and NIESTLÉ, NEUCHATEL and PARIS

TRANSLATION © EPWORTH PRESS 1967

FIRST ENGLISH EDITION PUBLISHED BY
EPWORTH PRESS 1967

Book Steward
FRANK H. CUMBERS

PRINTED AND BOUND IN ENGLAND BY
HAZELL WATSON AND VINEY LTD
AYLESBURY, BUCKS

Dedicated to the memory

of

GEORGES GODET

Me Fateri Non Pudet Multo
Obscuriorem Esse Hanc
Epistulam Quam Multas Alias

JOHANN SALOMO SEMLER

FOREWORD

THIS COMMENTARY, like all those of this series, takes it for granted that the reader has Nestlé's Greek New Testament in front of him, and when we depart from this text we point out the fact. Amongst other things, the commentary must justify the translation which is given, so that this should be read or re-read after studying the commentary. Words in square brackets in the translation have been added to facilitate comprehension of the text. In this commentary we have striven, like the writers of all this series, to give *non multa sed multum*; that is to say, from the immense literature about the Second Epistle to the Corinthians we have in each case chosen the most characteristic representatives of any particular important interpretation. The references have been duly checked, and in the few cases where citations have had to be made at second-hand we admit it. So as not to burden the exposition we have relegated to an appendix what we have to say about the idea of apostleship, or more precisely of the idea of the origin of the apostleship in the New Testament. May our translation and commentary help so far as possible in dissipating the mists which obscure this important Epistle!

CONTENTS

INTRODUCTION

A. The Problem of the Unity of the Epistle

THE AUTHENTICITY of the Second Epistle to the Corinthians has hardly been contested, although quotations from it probably do not occur before Marcion.[1] On the other hand, the problem of the unity of the Epistle has caused much ink to flow. It was the book by Hausrath, *Der Vierkapitelbrief des Paulus an die Korinther*, Heidelberg 1870, which really started it.[2] Hasrauth maintained two theses:

(*a*) 10–13 form a separate letter, mutilated at the beginning.

(*b*) This letter is identical with the one of which the Apostle speaks in 2⁴, written in sorrow and anxiety and with many tears.

These two contentions must, of course, be examined separately:

(*a*) In so far as the autonomy of the last four chapters is concerned, Hausrath's arguments are not all convincing; sometimes he tries to go too far. We will restrict ourselves to observations which seem to us important.

(i) The complete change of tone. 1–9 are addressed to a Church whose relations with the Apostle have passed through a profound crisis, but which has quietened down. The Apostle had received good news through Titus. The Church had taken a definite stand in opposition to some blameworthy person who had attacked the Apostle and his work in a particularly offensive way. Thus the sky had cleared. But suddenly, at the beginning of 10, the storm breaks. The Apostle is annoyed because the Corinthians have let themselves be taken in by alleged calumnies brought against him by false prophets. True enough, these people have already been mentioned, yet without the Apostle showing such indignation as to drive him to defend his apostleship in a diatribe well seasoned with sarcasm. He even lets himself go so far as 'playing the fool,' by urging with many details that he has suffered more than others.

Furthermore, the Apostle is very dissatisfied with the spirit which

---

[1] Cf. TERTULLIAN, *Adversus Marcionem* IV and V *passim* (*CSEL* 47). Among the few who deny the authenticity we may mention BRUNO BAUER, *Kritik der paulinischen Briefe* (1882), together with PIERSON and NABER, *Verisimilia* (1886). For the complicated hypothesis of H. DELAFOSSE (alias TURMEL), who finds extensive Marcionite and anti-Marcionite interpolations in the Epistles of Paul, cf. GOGUEL, *RHPR*, 1926, pp. 376ff and 1928 pp. 91ff. The commentaries of DELAFOSSE on 1 and 2 Corinthians have appeared in the series 'Christianisme' (Rieder, 1926 and 1927).

[2] But attention had already been drawn to the question by SEMLER, *Paraphrasis secundae epistulae ad Corinthios*, 1776, who separated 12¹⁴–13¹³ as a later codicil. Chapter 9 may equally well have been a separate note sent elsewhere than to Corinth ('to other cities of Achaia'). See the Preface in particular.

prevails at Corinth; cf. 12[20] where he reproves their jealousy, their disagreements and even the tendencies to apostasy. There had been no hint of such matters in 1–9.

(ii) The beginning of 10 is abrupt; there is no bridge to facilitate the transition. Even if one supposes, with E. Reuss, Michaelis and Jülicher,[3] that the dictation was interrupted between 9 and 10, this does not explain the radical change of tone and of the situation.

(b) The identification of the letter 10–13 with the Sorrowful Letter is not absolutely proved. Krenkel (*Beiträge zur Aufhellung der Geschichte und der Briefe des Apostles Paulus*, Brunswick 1895), followed by numerous scholars,[4] has maintained that 10 and 13 form a separate letter, but one *later* than 1–9. It was written following bad news which the Apostle had received in the meantime. These chapters, he says, do not really seem to be written 'in tears' but in a state of violent indignation. The notorious Sorrowful Letter, on the other hand, may have been intermediate between 1 Corinthians and 2 Corinthians, but it was lost.

Nevertheless, it is permissible to hold that letters must not be multiplied unless it is necessary, and that Hausrath's hypothesis, although not proved, is at least more plausible since tears and vexation are not incompatible with the tone the Apostle adopts. He may perhaps have wished to stress in 2[4] that the notorious letter had not been dictated *merely* with indignation.

In England, J. H. Kennedy arrived at completely similar conclusions, apparently without knowing Hausrath's work. See especially his book on *The Second and Third Epistles to the Corinthians*, London 1900, in which he treats 10–13 as a second (mutilated) Epistle and 1–9 as a third.[5]

We cannot, however, consider retracing the arguments here, except to say that Charles Bruston (cf. Bibliography), who accepts Krenkel's thesis, thinks that the Sorrowful Letter may not be lost, but may be identical with 1 Corinthians, the guilty party being the incestuous person of 1 Corinthians 5. It does not seem to us probable, since this affair happened at a much earlier date.

The unity of the Epistle has nevertheless been upheld by numerous

---

[3] E. REUSS (cf. Bibliography) pp. 285ff. MICHAELIS, *Einleitung in das Neue Testament*, 2nd edn, 1954, p. 180f. JÜLICHER, *Einleitung in das Neue Testament*, 1906, pp. 42ff.

[4] KRENKEL has been followed notably by CH. BRUSTON, WINDISCH, JÜLICHER-FASCHER, *Einleitung* 1931, p. 99. HAUSRATH's thesis (the identification of 10–13 with the Sorrowful Letter) has been adopted by SCHMIEDEL, *Handkommentar zum N.T.* II, 2nd edn, 1893, pp. 73–84; GOGUEL, *Introduction au Nouveau Testament*, vol. IV, pt 2; STRACHAN, in the Moffatt series of commentaries; JOHANNES WEISS, followed in part by GOGUEL, also identifies fragments of other letters in 2 Corinthians (see below).

[5] Cf. also the article by KENNEDY 'Are there two Epistles in 2 Corinthians?' in the *Expositor*, 1897, II (vol. 6) pp. 231ff and 285ff, as well as the same author's further developments in the periodical *Hermathena* (Dublin and London 1903, pp. 340ff) under the title 'The Problem of 2 Corinthians'.

scholars (beside those named in footnote 3), notably by Th.Zahn, *Einleitung* I, pp. 223ff, Georges Godet, *Commentaire*, Bachmann, *Kommentar*, Introduction, p. 3, Allo, *Commentaire*, A. Wikenhauser, *Einleitung in das Neue Testament* (Fribourg, Herder 1953), p. 282f.

Chapter **9** poses a problem, however, which is not solved by the independence given to **10** and **13**; for, as Semler noticed so long ago, not only is the trasition from **9** to **10** very awkward but also that from **8** to **9**. In fact, after the apparently completed recommendations about the collection given in **8** it is hard to understand why the Apostle re-opens the matter in **9** and—what is more significant—as if he had not previously mentioned it. We suggest the hypothesis that **9** formed a separate note which was taken by Titus to Corinth when he went there to set in motion the collection, as mentioned in **8**[6]. **9** would then also be prior to **1–8**. The fact that a visit is announced in the note (**9**[4]) would not have prevented Paul sending Titus again shortly before his visit, in the hope that when he came himself he might be able to gather together the sums of money ready for dispatch[6]

B. *The Journeys of the Apostle Paul*

According to 1 Corinthians 16[3–9], Paul already at the time of writing (A.D. 55 or 56) had the intention of making his way to Corinth in the near future. He sends Timothy on ahead (16[10]), which agrees very well with the information in the Acts (19[21–22]) according to which he sends Timothy and Erastus to Macedonia while he himself stays a little longer at Ephesus. We do not know whether Timothy actually arrived at Corinth. Subsequently the Apostle must have made his way there, though the Acts does not say so. This journey, often spoken of as the intermediate visit—because it occurs between 1 and 2 Corinthians, or, more precisely, between 1 Corinthians on the one hand and **10–13** on the other—or as the Sorrowful Visit, is duly attested by **12**[14], **13**[1–2], as well as **2**[1] (to refer only to indubitable texts). His stay there brought the Apostle grievous disappointment. Certainly the old contentions referred to in 1 Corinthians had been set at rest, but a new and most upsetting issue had arisen, as we have explained above.

The letter of **10–13** was therefore motivated by these new attacks upon the Apostle and his work. We do not know exactly where it was written. Goguel thinks at Ephesus, which is certainly possible though not certain. All that we can say is that at some time or other the Apostle returned to Asia, and doubtless that means to Ephesus. From

---

[6] It is well known that the Churches of Armenia have preserved an alleged Third Epistle of Paul to the Corinthians (of no value), preceded by an equally apocryphal letter from the Corinthians to the Apostle. Some parts are to be found in Latin manuscripts and in one Coptic manuscript, as well as in the Syriac Commentary of S. Ephrem on the Epistles of Paul. A retranslation of this correspondence into Greek (accompanied by some Latin fragments) has been given by A. HARNACK in the 'Kleine Texte' of H. LIETZMANN, no. 12 (1912).

there he set off again for Troas, where he stayed for some time. He waited there in vain for Titus, whom he had sent to Corinth, perhaps as bearer of the letter **10–13**. He then made his way into Macedonia, where he at last met his assistant who was bringing good news. The severe letter seemed to have had its effect. The only thing he was reproached for was not having returned again to Corinth as he had apparently promised. The Apostle explains at length his conduct in the matter. It is more difficult to understand why he now preferred to send yet another letter (**1–8**) before going himself to Corinth. We suggest that he wanted to leave Titus—the bearer of the note **9** as well as, subsequently, of the letter **1–8**—time to wind up the collection, the proceeds of which he himself wished to pick up as he went through Corinth before going on to Jerusalem. The last visit to Corinth, where he no doubt wrote the Epistle to the Romans, must, however, have taken place very soon after this, in view of the chronology of the life of the Apostle, according to which he arrived in Jerusalem at the end of A.D. 56 or the beginning of 57.[7]

Supplementary note

As we have already mentioned in our Commentary on the First Epistle to the Corinthians, Johannes Weiss and Maurice Goguel make a very detailed dissection of the two Corinthian Epistles. Although these hypotheses have not enjoyed great success, we mention them as a matter of information.

Johannes Weiss (*The History of Primitive Christianity*, ET 1937, I, pp. 323ff) isolates five letters:

(1) 1 Corinthians 10^{1-23}; 6^{12-20}; 11^{2-34}; $6^{14}-7^1$
(2) 1 Corinthians 7–9; $10^{24}-11^1$; 12–15; 16^{1-6}
(3) 1 Corinthians 1^1-6^{11}; Chapter 16 being apportioned between these three letters.
(4) An 'intervening letter' $2^{14}-6^{13}$; 7^{2-4}; **10–13**
(5) 1^1-2^{13}; 7^{5-16}; **9**

Maurice Goguel (*Introduction au Nouveau Testament*, IV, 2, p. 86) finds six letters:

(1) $6^{14}-7^1$; 1 Corinthians 6^{12-20}; 10^{1-22}
(2) 1 Corinthians 5^1-6^{11}; 7^1-8^{13}; $10^{23}-14^{40}$; 15^{1-58}; $16^{1-9, 12}$
(3) 1 Corinthians $1^{10}-4^{21}$; 9^{1-27}; 16^{10-11} (other elements undeterminable)
(4) 10^1-13^{10} ('Intermediate Letter')
(5) 1^1-6^{13}; 7^2-8^{24}
(6) 9^{1-15}

---

[7] For chronology cf. GOGUEL, *Introduction* IV, 1, Chapter 2.—An interesting article by W. C. VAN UNNICK on the journeys of the Apostle Paul, and of which we have taken account in the Commentary, appeared in *Studia Paulina in honorem J. de Zwaan* (Haarlem 1953) under the title 'Reisepläne und Amen-Sagen, Zusammenhang und Gedankenfolge in II Kor. 1.15–24' (pp. 215–34).

We agree with M. Goguel over the contents of the 'Intermediate Letter'; we ourselves separate 9 from the remainder of the Epistle, but put this note before 1-8.

It is only fair to say that F. Spitta, in his lecture courses before 1914, had already suggested similar views, though we have found no trace of them in his published works.

C. Notes on the Form of the Text

The text called Alexandrine is represented by the following manuscripts: S (Sinaiticus), B (Vaticanus), both complete; and C (Codex Ephraemi), a palimpsest which is not wholly legible.

The Western text is given particularly by D_2, sometimes denoted Dp (Claromontanus), which has few lacunae; by E_3 (Sangermanensis); by F_2 (Augiensis); and by G_3 (Boernerianus). This form of the text is supported in general by the Latin versions and by citations of the Fathers of the 2nd and 3rd centuries.

Papyrus p 46 (of the Chester Beatty collection), which dates from the 3rd century, gives a text (the 'Caesarean'?) intermediate between the 'Alexandrine' and 'Western' texts.

Codex A (Alexandrinus) lacks 4^{13}-12^7. There is lack of agreement about the exact character of this text.

The Byzantine text is given by K^2 (Mosquensis), and by L^2 (Angelicus), and by the great mass of minuscules.

BIBLIOGRAPHICAL COMMENTS

A. Editions of the Text

E. NESTLÉ, *Novum Testamentum graece*, 22nd edn, Stuttgart 1956.

C. TISCHENDORF, *Novum Testamentum graece*, ed. Octava maior II, 1872.

RAHLFS, *Septuaginta*, 2 vols, Stuttgart 1935 (containing the Apocrypha).

R. STIER and K. G. W. THEILE, *Polyglotten-Bibel*, Bielefeld 1863 et seq. Always very useful. Gives for the O.T.: Hebrew, Greek, Latin, German; and for the N.T.: Greek, Latin and German.

R. H. CHARLES, *Apocrypha and Pseudepigrapha*, 2 vols, Oxford 1913.

KAUTZSCH, *Apokryphen und Pseudepigraphen*, Tübingen 1900.

J. LABOURT and P. BATTIFOL, *Les Odes de Salomon* (in French), Paris 1911.

F. MARTIN, *Le livre d'Henoch* (translation of the Ethiopic), Paris 1906.

H. VAILLANT, *Le livre des Secrets d'Hénoch* (2 Enoch). Slavonic text and French translation, Paris 1952.

L. GOLDSCHMIDT, *Der babylonische Talmud* (German translation), small edition in 12 vols, Berlin 1930–6.

FREEDMANN, *Midrasch Rabba*, English translation in 10 vols, London 1939.

L. COHN and P. WENDLAND, *Philonis opera*, (a) large edition with Index, 1896, in 8 vols, (b) small edition, 1896, in 12 vols.

Griechische Christliche Schriftsteller (*GCS*), edited by the Berlin Academy.

MIGNE, *Patrologia*, Greek and Latin series (*MPG, MPL*).

Corpus Scriptorum Ecclesiasticorum Latinorum (*CSEL*), edited by the Vienna Academy.

B. Dictionaries and Grammars

HENRY ESTIENNE, *Thesaurus Linguae Graecae*, 5 vols, 1572. Impression by Didot 1831.

PREUSCHEN–BAUER, *A Greek–English Lexicon of the New Testament and Other Early Christian Literature*, translation and adaptation of 4th German edition by W. F. ARNDT and F. W. GINGRICH, Cambridge and Chicago 1957.

LIDDELL–SCOTT, *Greek–English Lexicon*, 2nd edn London 1925–40.

J. H. MOULTON and G. MILLIGAN, *The Vocabulary of the Greek N.T.*, London 1930.

J. H. MOULTON, *A Grammar of N.T. Greek*, vol. 2, ed W. F. HOWARD, London 1930.

BLASS–DEBRUNNER, translation and revision of the 9th–10th German edn by R. W. FUNK, *A Greek Grammar of the N.T. and Other Early Christian Literature*, Cambridge and Chicago 1961.

L. RADEMACHER, *Neutestamentliche Grammatik* 1912 (in the Lietzmann Handbuch zum N.T.).

ALEXANDRE WESTPHAL, *Dictionnaire encyclopédique de la Bible*, I, Paris 1932; II, Valence 1935 (new edn in preparation). Contains the articles by H. Clavier on Paul and on the Epistles to the Corinthians.

Vocabulary of the Bible, ed J.-J. von Allmen, ET London 1958.

PAULY–WISSOWA, *Realenzyklopädie des klassischen Altertums*, 1894 et seq. This monumental encyclopaedia, perhaps too little used by theologians, contains not only detailed articles on classical antiquity, but also on Palestine and surrounding countries.

Theologisches Wörterbuch zum N.T., ed G. Kittel and then G. Friedrich (Stuttgart).

C. Some Commentaries

ST JOHN CHRYSOSTOM, Sermons on the 2nd Epistle of Paul to the Corinthians, *MPG*, 61.

CALVIN, *Commentary on the N.T.* (a) Latin text in Opera Calvini (in the Corpus Reformatorum), vol. 49; (b) *Calvin: the Second Epistle of Paul the Apostle to the Corinthians and the Epistles to Timothy, Titus and Philemon*, trans. T. A. Smail, Edinburgh 1964.

JOHANN ALBRECHT BENGEL, *Gnomon Novi Testamenti*, 1742, 3rd edn 1773. We have used an impression of the 3rd edn printed in Berlin 1855. The German edition should not be used.

J. J. WETSTENIUS (WETTSTEIN), *Hē kainē Diathēkē*, 2nd vol., Amsterdam 1752, pp. 177–215.

A. SCHLATTER, *Erläuterungen zum N.T.*, II (1909), pp. 334–436.

EDOUARD REUSS, *La Bible*. N.T. 3rd part, vol. I, 1878, pp. 279–355.

H. LIETZMANN, in the Handbuch zum N.T. for which he was also editor, 2nd edn 1923, 3rd edn 1928, 4th edn 1949.

GEORGES GODET, Neuchâtel 1914, *Commentaire* published posthumously by Paul Comtesse. This writer must never be cited without his Christian name, particularly in connection with introductory matters concerning this Epistle. For it is then often difficult to know whether the reference is to the above commentary by GEORGES GODET or to the *Introduction au N.T.* by FRÉDÉRIC GODET, 1st part: *Les épîtres pauliniennes* (Paris 1893).

CH. BRUSTON, *Les trois épîtres de l'apôtre Paul aux Corinthiens conservées par l'Eglise* (Paris 1917).

FR ALLO, in the collection 'Etudes bibliques', published by Lecoffre-Gabalda, 1937.

PH. BACHMANN in the 'Theologischer Kommentar zum N.T.,' founded by Th. Zahn, vol. 8, 4th edn 1922.

H. WINDISCH in 'Kritisch-Exegetischer Kommentar zum N.T.',

founded by H. A. W. Meyer (1924). Along with ALLO the most complete commentary.

A. PLUMMER, in the International Critical Commentary, 1915, new edn 1925.

R. H. STRACHAN, in the Moffatt N.T. Commentary, 1935, 4th edn 1946.

H. STRACK and P. BILLERBECK, *Kommentar zum N.T. aus Talmud und Midrasch*, 1922 et seq.

D. Introductions and Monographs

FRÉDÉRIC GODET, *Introduction au N.T.*, 1st part, Paris 1893.

M. GOGUEL, *Introduction au N.T.*, vol. 4 (in 2 parts): 'Les Épîtres pauliniennes,' 1925-6.

ALFRED WIKENHAUSER, *Einleitung in das N.T.*, Fribourg-in-Brisgau 1953.

WILHELM MICHAELIS, *Einleitung in das N.T.*, 2nd edn, revised, Berne 1954.

F. PRAT, *La théologie de saint Paul*, the latest edition appears to have been 1949.

ALBERT SCHWEITZER, *Die Mystik des Apostels Paulus*, Tübingen 1930; ET London 1931 (*The Mysticism of Paul the Apostle*).

W. D. DAVIES, *Paul and Rabbinic Judaism*, London 1939 (cited as: Davies).

Details of the many other works referred to in the Commentary will be given when the reference is made.

E. Modern Translations referred to by Abbreviations

B.d.Cent.: *La Bible du Centenaire*, edited by the Société Biblique de Paris. The N.T. has been printed separately: M. GOGUEL and H. MONNIER, *Le Nouveau Testament*, Paris 1929.

Synodale Version: *La Version Synodale*, published by the Société biblique de France.

CRAMPON: *La Sainte Bible* by Canon CRAMPON, Paris 1952.

OSTY: The (excellent!) translation by E. OSTY in the *Bible de Jérusalem* (full title: 'La Sainte Bible traduite en français sous la direction de l'Ecole Biblique de Jérusalem'), Paris 1956.

WILLIAMS: C. K. WILLIAMS, *The New Testament. A new translation in plain English*, London 1952.

FENTON: F. FENTON, *The Holy Bible in Modern English*.

ABBREVIATIONS

ATANT   *Abhandlungen zur Theologie des Alten und des Neuen Testaments*
ARW   *Archiv für Religionswissenschaft*
BZAW   *Beihefte zur Zeitschrift für die alttestamentliche Wissenschaft*
BZNW   *Beihefte zur Zeitschrift für die neutestamentliche Wissenschaft*
CNT   *Commentaire du Nouveau Testament*
CT   *Cahiers théologiques de l'actualité protestante*
CSEL   *Corpus Scriptorum Ecclesiasticorum Latinorum*
DACL   *Dictionnaire d'archéologie chrétienne et de liturgie*
DEB   *Dictionnaire encyclopédique de la Bible*
DTC   *Dictionnaire de théologie catholique*
EB   *Encyclopaedia Biblica*
EHPR   *Etudes d'histoire et de philosophie religieuses* (Strasbourg)
EJ   *Encyclopaedia Judaïca*
ERE   *Encyclopaedia of Religion and Ethics*
ETR   *Etudes théologiques et religieuses* (Montpellier)
ET   *Expository Times*
GCS   *Die griechischen christlichen Schriftsteller der ersten drei Jahrhunderte*
HDB   *Hastings Dictionary of the Bible*
HTR   *Harvard Theological Review*
JBL   *Journal of Biblical Literature*
JR   *Journal of Religion*
JTS   *Journal of Theological Studies*
Jud.   *Judaica*
MPG   *Migne, Patrology, Greek Series*
MPL   *Migne, Patrology, Latin Series*
RAC   *Reallexikon für Antike und Christentum*
RB   *Revue biblique*
RE   *Realenzyklopädie für protestantische Theologie und Kirche,* 3rd edn
RGG   *Die Religion in Geschichte und Gegenwart,* 2nd edn
REG   *Revue des études grecques*
REJ   *Revue des études juives*
RHPR   *Revue d'histoire et de philosophie religieuses* (Strasbourg)
RHR   *Revue de l'histoire des religions*
RKAW   *Realenzyklopädie der klassischen Altertumswissenschaften*
RTP   *Revue de théologie et de philosophie* (Lausanne)
SAB   *Sitzungsberichte der Preussischen Akademie der Wissenschaften zu Berlin (phil.-hist. Klasse)*

TB	*Theologische Blätter*
TLZ	*Theologische Literatur-Zeitung*
TR	*Theologische Rundschau*
TS	*Theologische Studien*
TSK	*Theologische Studien und Kritiken*
TWNT	*Theologisches Wörterbuch zum Neuen Testament*
TZ	*Theologische Zeitschrift*
TU	*Texte und Untersuchungen zur Geschichte der altchristlichen Literatur*
ZAW	*Zeitschrift für die alttestamentliche Wissenschaft*
ZKG	*Zeitschrift für Kirchengeschichte*
ZNTW	*Zeitschrift für die neutestamentliche Wissenschaft*
ZST	*Zeitschrift für systematische Theologie*
ZTK	*Zeitschrift für Theologie und Kirche*

CHAPTER I

(1) *Paul, Apostle of Christ Jesus by the will of God, and brother Timothy, to the Church of God which is at Corinth, as well as to all Christians to be found in the whole of Greece, (2) grace and peace to you from God our Father and from the Lord Jesus Christ.*

1[1] For the word '*apostolos*'='apostle' see the Appendix. According to Acts 16[1] Timothy came from Lystra, and his mother was already a Christian when Paul arrived there. According to 2 Timothy 1[5] his grandmother was likewise a Christian; but it was Paul who made Timothy a preacher of the gospel. Their association was very close. To judge from 1 and 2 Timothy Paul even made him something like an inspector of various Churches. He praises him in Philippians 2[19-22] and 1 Corinthians 4[17], where he calls him his dear son, faithful in the Lord. Even if we leave aside the Pastoral Epistles, it is clear that Paul sometimes committed to him heavy responsibilities. He left him for some time at Philippi, together with Sosthenes, as his representative (Acts 17[14,15]; cf. 18[5]). According to 1 Corinthians 4[17] and 16[10] he sent Timothy (or intended to send him?) to Corinth on an important mission. It is curious that 2 Corinthians makes no mention of it. If Timothy had failed in his mission, Paul would certainly have defended him. One can only think that this visit was already relatively long past, a year and a half to two years earlier. But as Allo rightly observes, we are so ill-informed that we do not even know whether Timothy actually reached Corinth.

Timothy is also named as a collaborator in the Letters to the Philippians, the Colossians, in 1 and 2 Thessalonians (along with Silas) and to Philemon. He is never called an Apostle, but a 'brother', i.e. a Christian brother.[1] The first person plural, which is very often used in our Epistle (and in others), does not necessarily imply that Timothy actually participated in its composition. It can be an epistolary plural, a kind of 'plural of modesty.'

'*Sun tois hagiois*' = 'as well as to all the saints,' etc., shows that this was a circular letter. Achaia comprised central Greece and the Peloponnese. We do not know where Churches (or scattered Christians) may have been, apart from Corinth, Cenchreae (Rom 16[1]) and Athens (Acts 17[34]).

---

[1] Other references to Timothy are: Acts 20[4]; Romans 16[21]; 1 Thessalonians 3[2,6]; Hebrews 13[23].

(3) *Blessed be the God and Father of our Lord Jesus Christ, the compassionate Father and the God of all comfort.* (4) *He it is who pours comfort over all our afflictions, in such a way that we can comfort others in their afflictions by the comfort which we ourselves receive from God.* (5) *For as the sufferings of Christ extend to us abundantly, so also our comfort abounds through Christ.*

1[2] The formula '*charis kai eirēnē*' = 'grace and peace' is found at the beginning of all the Epistles (1 and 2 Tim add '*eleos*' = 'mercy'). It unites in one the Greek salutation ('*chaire*') and the Hebrew ('*šalôm*'), both taking a religious significance which the ending of the verse emphasises.

1[3] opens with a brief doxology, 'Blessed be God', etc. ('*eulogētos ho theos*', etc.), the first three words of which reproduce the formula used by Jews whenever they speak of God.

Here again God is called 'the Father of our Lord Jesus Christ, the Father of mercies[2] and God of all consolation.'

1[3-11] is explained by the tribulations which Paul had endured and which do not seem to have ended, and in addition also by those of his recipients. He calls them '*thlipseis*' and '*pathēmata*' = 'tribulations' and 'sufferings'. According to 1[8] they were unbearable and brought even threat of death. We do not know whether some severe illness was the trouble, or a recrudescence of persecution by Jews or Gentiles. What is more important is to grasp how, in all his sufferings, Paul found such consolation in attachment to Christ that he must in some measure share his sufferings with the Corinthians.

This leads us to the problem of ascertaining why he here considers that his tribulations were a way of suffering with Christ. In 1[5] he even speaks of the sufferings of Christ Himself, in which he participates. It is this attitude that Windisch and Albert Schweitzer call 'Christ mysticism.'

Now we know that in apocalyptic Judaism woes are predicted which will precede the messianic kingdom, and that the sufferings of the faithful can guarantee their salvation (cf. 2 Esd 7[6-16]).[3] However, for Paul as for Mark (Ch. 13), these sufferings naturally do not announce the arrival of the Messiah on earth but his glorious return and the commencement of the Kingdom of God. That the Messiah himself should suffer is indeed inconceivable in the Judaism of this period.[4] For Christians the cross of Christ is above all an historical

[2] This expression recalls Wisdom 9[1]: '*Kurios tou eleous*'= 'Lord of mercy'. *Oiktirmoi*' ('mercies') = '*rahamîm*' frequently in the O.T.

[3] Other texts in STRACK-BILLERBECK, I, p. 195.—The passage in 2 Esdras teaches that there are two ways, one narrow and one broad. But they are successive: the faithful who have travelled the sorrowful way here below will reach the other in heaven.

[4] See the classical study by G. DALMAN, *Der leidende und sterbende Messias der Synagoge im ersten nachchristlichen Jahrtausend*, Berlin 1888, and our article: 'Messie juif et Messie chrétien', *RHPR* 1938, pp. 819ff.

(6) *If we are afflicted, it is for your consolation and salvation;
if we are comforted, again it is for your consolation, which proves
its efficacy in the endurance of the same sufferings which we ourselves undergo.* (7) *And our hope concerning you is well-founded; for
we know that as you are associated with our sufferings, so are you also
with our comfort.* (8) *Indeed, we would not leave you ignorant, brothers,
about the affliction which came upon us in Asia, that we have been ex-
ceedingly overwhelmed, beyond our powers, so that we despaired even of
life.* (9) *But in our innermost heart we have accepted the sentence of
death, that we may have no confidence in ourselves but in God who
raises the dead.* (10) *He it is who saved us from so cruel a death,
and who still saves us; in Him we have placed our hope, that He will
save us in the future.* (11) *And you also bring your aid to assist us by
prayer, so that this boon may be granted me through the prayer of
intercession made for me by many Christians in the presence of numerous witnesses.*

fact, and it is this which allows the Apostle to give a quite special
significance to the tribulations of a Christian. Christians can be
saved to the extent in which they accept suffering with Him. By so
doing they are raised with Him. This does not imply that the heavenly
Christ continues to suffer; but the Christian must reproduce in some
way the sufferings of the earthly Christ in his 'body', that is, in his
material existence, so that the old Adam may be slain (cf. Rom 6,
especially v. 6). It is this which permits Albert Schweitzer to say that
Pauline mysticism is like eschatology viewed from within.[5] The pas-
sion and resurrection of Christ are in effect eschatological facts,
because they prepare for the end, and all this is put into relation with
the concept of the Church, the body of Christ; for the existence of the
Christian must never be separated from that of the Church. It is this,
no doubt, which explains the curious remark in Colossians 1[24]: 'I
complete in my flesh the afflictions of Christ.'

But why should these comparatively normal tribulations have
seemed sometimes to terrify the Apostle, especially according to
1 Corinthians 4[9]? It was doubtless not because he feared death in
itself, but he was afraid of a premature ending to his mission among
the Gentiles which God had committed to him and which itself represented one element in the eschatological drama. For, according to
Paul, the Gospel must be proclaimed to the Gentiles before the Jews
would be converted and the end come.[6] However, we must remember
that the Apostle Paul never gives us a genuine synthesis of his doctrine of this matter. He leaves us merely to catch a glimpse of his
fundamental ideas, which are, moreover, very well summarised in 1
Peter 4[13] and 5[1].

[5] *The Mysticism of Paul the Apostle*, ET London 1931, pp. 112–13, and our
article 'De H. J. Holtzmann à Albert Schweitzer', in *Ehrfurcht vor dem Leben*,
symposium for A. Schweitzer, Berne 1955, pp. 21–9.
[6] Romans 11[25].—O. CULLMANN, *RHPR* 1936, pp. 210–45, even thinks that
the notorious '*katechōn*' may be Paul himself, which appears to us less likely.

In the matter of 'Christ mysticism,' as is well known, Loisy and others[7] lay much stress on parallels which may be found in the mystery religions, which promise the initiate union with a god. But to conclude from this that there was any influence of these religions upon Paulinism is a long stride to take. For no trace of eschatology is found in these religions. Let us say, rather, that Christianity was able to actualise some of the aspirations which gleamed through these mysteries. And we must remember that never in Christianity is the believer identified with Christ, in the way the believer in the Hellenistic religions was sometimes identified with his god ('I am Osiris').[8]

1[3-11] Paul speaks of some great affliction. The important thing is to understand how he interprets it. '*Paraklēsis*' can be translated 'consolation' (NEB) or 'comfort' (AV, RV). If a distinction has to be made between '*thlipseis*' and '*pathēmata*', we may with Bengel render these nouns by '*angusta animi*' and '*adversa*' respectively.[9]

According to **1[4]** it is God who comforts ('*hupo tou theou*') and according to **1[5]** the consolation is efficacious through Christ as intermediary ('*dia tou Christou*'). As always, '*perisseuein*' means 'to abound'; the sufferings of Christ in some way overflow 'unto us'. On the other hand, the comfort the Apostle receives is so abundant that the Corinthians also may profit by it through the medium of the body of Christ to which all belong.

1[6] The beginning of the verse is difficult. How can Paul's affliction serve not only for the consolation of the Corinthians, but also for their salvation ('*kai sōtērias*')? We do not believe that a kind of substitute suffering is in mind. The Apostle is thinking of the endurance ('*hupomonē*') which his consolations produce. '*Energeisthai*' means, in effect, 'to work' or 'show to be effective' (cf. 'energetic'). The second sense fits here. Strachan gives the good rendering 'which is effective as it nerves you to endure,' etc.[10]

---

[7] Cf. particularly A. Loisy, *Les mystères païens et le Mystère chrétien*, 2nd edn 1930, and R. Reitzenstein, *Die hellenistischen Mysterienreligionen*, 3rd edn 1927.

[8] Cf. A. Schweitzer, *Paul and his Interpreters*, ET, London 1912.

[9] H. H. Farmer has written some fine pages on the passage 1[3-5] in his book *The Healing Cross*, London 1938, pp. 133ff. Even so he has not stressed the difficulty created by souls who seem to refuse all consolation—on the one hand, rebellious men (and there is a good deal of anti-God attitude among the self-styled godless), and on the other hand, by the despairing. It is true that the Apostle does not mention them in this passage; yet he knew them, and it is doubtless to them that he directs his moving appeal 'Be reconciled to God' (5[20]). And it is certain that to render the appeal effective he used the *ultima ratio* of Christians—the prayer of intercession.

[10] For '*energeō*' cf. the article by K. W. Clark, 'The meaning of *energeō* and *katargeō* in the N.T.', *JBL* 1935, pp. 93–101. According to Clark, Paul's use of '*energeō*' always hints at a supernatural power animating the Christian; cf. *TWNT* II, pp. 649ff.

1⁷ gives classical formulation to the principle of this 'Pauline mysticism.'

1⁸ '*Exaporēthēnai*' = 'to despair' is rare in the Bible (here and 4⁸, as well as LXX Psalm 87¹⁶). It is a kind of paroxysm of anguish which banishes all hope. '*Bareō*' = 'to load.' According to Chrysostom¹¹ the word evokes the image of an overladen ship.¹² The almost pleonastic use of language to depict the intensity of the suffering will also be observed: 'excessively' ('*kath*' *huperbolēn*') and 'beyond our powers' ('*huper dunamin*').

1⁹ᵃ '*Eschēkamen*' has been variously translated 'accept', 'pronounce', 'understand'. We have not been able to convince ourselves that '*echō*' could mean 'pronounce' (i.e. pronounce sentence), so the choice lies between 'understand' and 'accept'. If we adopt the latter interpretation it is because the context suggests it.¹³ The Apostle has ceased rebelling against the idea of his premature death; he has therefore accepted the sentence of death in his innermost heart.

1⁹ᵇ⁻¹⁰ 'God who raises the dead' is identical with a phrase found in the 'Eighteen Benedictions.'¹⁴ It may have been suggested by Deuteronomy 32³⁹ LXX ('I will kill and I will make alive,' i.e. resurrect) or by 1 Kings 2⁶ LXX (the same, but in the present tense).¹⁵

The typically Jewish custom of linking sickness with death is well known, and of calling recovery resurrection.¹⁶ The danger of death is characterised as particularly serious by the pronoun '*tēlikoutos*' = 'such a one', 'so great a one'. It could be translated (with Strachan) as 'a death so terrible.'¹⁷

---

¹¹ *MPG* 61, col. 394.
¹² Are these dangers of death the same as those referred to in 1 Corinthians 15³²? One has the impression, rather, that it is some more recent event. Is it the riot related in Acts 19 which is being alluded to here (or in 1 Corinthians 15³²)? It is impossible to tell.
¹³ As Calvin explains: 'I thought my death fixed and decided.'
¹⁴ The Hebrew text of this famous prayer is found in J. DALMAN, *Worte Jesu*, I, p. 299. A French translation in J. LAGRANGE, *Le judaïsme avant Jésus-Christ*, 1931, p. 466. STRACK–BILLERBECK give a German translation in their commentary, IV, 1, p. 211.
¹⁵ The Hebrew of Deuteronomy 32³⁹ uses the Imperfect; 1 Samuel 2⁶ has participles.
¹⁶ Cf. Psalm 85⁷; Psalm 119²⁵ and passim; and especially Hosea 6², cf. E. JACOB, *Theology of the Old Testament*, ET 1958, p. 308.
¹⁷ ALLO: 'Such a prolonged death,' which would doubtless mean 'a danger of death which was so prolonged.' The translation is possible philologically, though in this case the Apostle would probably have written '*ek tēlikoutōn thanatōn*' (cf. the use of the plural '*thanatoi*' in 11²³ below). After '*errhusato hēmas*' we read '*rhuetai*', following the Textus Receptus and Vulgate. '*Kai rhusetai*', given by the majority of other witnesses and adopted by Nestlé, may be a repetition of the '*kai eti rhusetai*' at the end of the verse.

1¹¹ The Apostle makes use of the circumstances to forge a strange link of prayer with the people of Corinth, from whom he is absent. The Corinthians will pray for him, as **1¹¹ᵃ** clearly implies (up to *'deēsei'* = 'by prayer'). Yet something more is probably meant than a simple prayer of intercession. The passage in 1 Corinthians 5⁴, where Paul speaks of his spiritual presence during his (physical) absence, is significant in this connection.

The second half of v. 11 gives the impression of being overloaded (Windisch: 'a fussy mode of expression'; Plummer: 'a perplexing sentence'[18]). The expression *'ek pollōn prosōpōn* (?)' = 'by many people (?)' seems superfluous preceding *'dia pollōn'* ('by many people') at the end of the verse. Likewise the redundancy of *'eis hēmas'* = 'for us' and *'huper hēmōn'*[19] (same meaning) is odd.

But it is not merely the style which is difficult. Without any known exception all the translators take *'eucharistein'* in the sense of 'to give thanks, return thanks'; then the statement 'so that God may be thanked by many Christians for the gracious favour (*'charisma'*) granted to the Apostle' must be understood. Why should the giving of thanks be represented as the aim, or in some way the essential feature, of the operation?

To resolve this difficulty we observe first of all that *'eucharistein'* can very well mean 'to request' (in general)[20] or even 'to bestow a favour.'[21] Strangely enough, both meanings are applicable in this passage. The Corinthians will bestow a favour (*'charisma'*) on the Apostle. But underlying there is the idea of 'to pray'—for it is by their prayers that the bestowal takes place. Thus we arrive at the following translation: 'in order that the favour which you do me (*"to eis hēmas charisma"*) may be bestowed through the prayers of many people (*"dia pollōn eucharistēthē"*).'[22] The sense seems clearer and more natural in this way.

The stylistic difficulties remain. Consider first the expression *'ek pollōn prosōpōn,'* which seems to duplicate *'dia pollōn,'* remembering that *'prosōpon'* in the sense of 'person' (the meaning presupposed by the traditional translation) is unknown to both Old and New

---

[18] BACHMANN translates: 'Whilst you also render service on our behalf through prayer, so that from many faces the manifestation of grace which flows unto us may be extolled in connection with us.' If gibberish were not too harsh a word we might use it of this!

[19] Some texts read *'huper humōn'*; but it is an error.

[20] Judith 8²⁵, where the verb *'eucharistein'* is used for a prayer which is a request for deliverance.

[21] Cf. LIDDELL-SCOTT.

[22] Putting the phrase in the active we have *'charisma eucharistein'*, which is a good Greek construction of an intransitive verb governing the accusative of an internal object (the content or result of the action), cf. 'to live a life', 'to fight a fight', etc.

(12) *For this is what we boast about—the witness of our con-science [which assures us] that it is in holiness and religious purity, not in worldly wisdom, but by the grace of God, that we have conducted ourselves in the world, and more especially in relation to you.* (13) *For we write nothing to you but what you can clearly read and understand.*

Testaments,[23] where it always means 'the face, the countenance.'[24] Bachmann translates 'from many faces,' which would be an odd ex-pression to use.

To clarify the problem we first observe that two other readings are extant,[25] of which *'en prosōpō pollōn'* = 'in the presence of many people' seems the more interesting though the less well attested. For here *'prosōpon'* has its usual meaning 'face', and *'en prosōpō'* = 'in front of' is a current biblical expression.[26] We must assume that the many people present, not all of whom could make verbal contribution to this volume of prayer, must have united themselves inwardly to the prayers and given them, so to speak, more resonance.[27]

1[12] *'Kauchēsis'* denotes not only the act of bragging or boasting, but also its cause, i.e. the subject of boasting (*'kauchēma'*). *'Suneidēsis'*, as already amongst certain philosophers, definitely connotes the 'con-science', which sometimes accuses and sometimes acquits, cf. Romans 2[15].[28] Here his conscience acquits the Apostle by testifying to his

---

[23] On the meaning of this noun in secular literature, cf. MAURICE NÉDONCELLE, 'Prosopon et Persona dans l'Antiquité classique,' *Revue des sciences religieuses*, 1948, pp. 277–99.

[24] The term *'prosōpolēmpsia'*, occurring in the N.T., which is translated as 'respect of persons', could not prove the contrary, because here again the force of *'prosōpon'* which is presupposed is 'face' or 'head'.

[25] *'En pollō prosōpō,'* principally in p 46, G, M; and *'en prosōpō pollōn,'* only in some Greek minuscules and one old Latin manuscript.

[26] It is naturally fashioned on the Hebrew *'lipᵉney'*. Moreover, it should be noted that this reading can explain the origin of the others by errors of dictation or copying, under the influence of the *'dia pollōn'*, the meaning of which has been able to colour the phrase under discussion.

[27] The question can still be asked whether the reading to which we have given preference, because it seems to us the most ancient, was not already itself the result of a corruption. The parallel passage already mentioned in 1 Corinthians 5[4] in fact calls for something which would correspond to *'sunachthentōn humōn'* ('when you are assembled together'). Now, emending *'prosōpō'* to *'prosodō'* would be enough to procure this meaning, for *'prosodos'* signifies the act of going to an assembly and also the gathering itself (cf. ESTIENNE: *Thesaurus*). *'En prosodō pollōn'* would then mean: 'when the whole company is assembled.'

[28] Cf. the texts of Seneca cited by Windisch and particularly the article by HENRI CLAVIER, 'La notion de "*suneidēsis*", pierre de touche de l'hellénisme de l'apôtre Paul,' in *Volume jubilaire du 1900ᵉ anniversaire de la visite de saint Paul en Grèce*, Athens 1953.—Judaism does not seem to have had a special term for what the Greeks called *'suneidēsis'*; but *'leḇ'* often has the same sense. Cf. STRACK-BILLERBECK, III, pp. 92ff.

8 II CORINTHIANS

(14) *Indeed, I hope that as you already partially understand me, you will ultimately understand me completely; because in the day of our Lord Jesus we shall be a matter of commendation for you, as you will be for us.*

disinterestedness.—'*Hagiotēs*' = 'holiness' is basically an attribute of God. Used here of Christians, the term has an untypical moral connotation. In general it is a religious term, signifying dedication to Christ (cf. '*hoi hagioi*' = 'the saints,' i.e. 'Christians').—'*Eilikrinia*' is used in the Wisdom books as a divine attribute (Wis 7²⁵). Paul uses it here to mean the virtue of 'purity', and, in particular, the purity of his intentions.²⁹ Both these qualities are the work of God ('*tou theou*'), cf. 1 Corinthians 5⁸ and here 2¹⁷. '*Sophia sarkikē*' = 'fleshly wisdom' recalls the '*sarkikoi*' and '*sarkinoi*' = 'fleshly men' of 1 Corinthians 3¹⁻³, as well as the 'wisdom of this world' of 1 Corinthians 1²⁰, 2⁶. In the latter passages he puts it in opposition to the '*sophia theou*' = 'wisdom of God' or 'wisdom which comes from God'; here, he puts it in opposition to the grace of God.³⁰

1¹³ Strachan translates: 'you don't have to read between the lines of my letters.' But what follows shows that the accusation was more weighty. It seems that he was reproached for saying the opposite of what he thought ('*alla graphomen*', etc.). '*Graphomen*' = 'we write' must refer to all the letters; '*ē kai epiginōskete*' is lacking in p 46 and B, though it is not necessarily an interpolation. If the words are retained, the translation must run 'what you read ('*anaginōskete*') and understand ('*epiginōskete*') or, to imitate the play on words, 'what you apprehend and comprehend' (namely, from my letters).³¹

The 'comprehension' implies also an appreciation of Paul's intentions, which the Corinthians still perceive only partially ('*apo merous*'). The hope is ('*elpizō*') that they will come to a full comprehension. The whole passage, moreover, is slightly reminiscent in its phraseology of 1 Corinthians 13¹²ᵇ.

1¹⁴ The reciprocity of the subjects of 'glorification' (you are my pride and I am yours) is emphatic, and it is made clear that both parties will play a part on 'the day of our Lord Jesus Christ,' i.e. on the day of judgement.³²

²⁹ The adjective '*eilikrinēs*' is found again in Philippians 1¹⁰.
³⁰ The two kinds of wisdom have, from one angle, been well characterised by WILLIAM BLAKE: 'The fox provides for himself, but God provides for the lion,' in *Proverbs of Hell*, 1908; cf. complete edition of his works by G. KEYNES, Bloomsbury (*sic*) 1927, p. 194.
³¹ According to CH. BRUSTON the phrase means: we write nothing else to you but what you read in the Scriptures. An original if not convincing interpretation.
³² 'Day of the Lord' = the day of judgement in many O.T. passages. See our commentary on *The First Epistle of Saint Paul to the Corinthians*, ET 1961, p. 3. For the congregation regarded as a 'subject for pride' see also 1 Corinthians 15³¹.

(15, 16) *It was with this assurance that I intended to come first of all to you, so that you had a second opportunity for rejoicing. In fact, I wanted to visit you on my way to Macedonia, and to return to you when I left Macedonia, to be accompanied by you to Judaea.* (17) *Did I show levity in making this plan? Or were my intentions inspired by merely human motives, so that I am found saying 'Yes' and 'No' in the same breath?*

1¹²⁻¹⁴ therefore open up a sort of apology, whereby the Apostle protests his sincerity. It continues in v.15, where one definite misunderstanding is cleared aside: since the Apostle had not been able to keep his promise to return to Corinth,[33] his adversaries had profited from his default to accuse him of making airy promises (*'elaphria'* v. 17 = 'levity').

1¹⁵⁻¹⁶ The expression 'with this assurance' (*'tautē tē pepoithēsei'*) must refer to the whole passage 1¹²⁻¹⁴, the assurance being given by his good conscience.—*'Proteron'* = 'first' belongs to *'elthein'* = 'to come'. The Apostle had reckoned on visiting Corinth before the other Churches, doubtless by crossing the Aegean Sea. That would have afforded the Corinthians a subsequent second privilege (*'deutera charis'*),[34] namely, that of receiving a further visit when he returned from the journey to Macedonia (*'palin'* = in returning or in retracing his steps[35]).

'Propemphthēnai' does not merely mean 'to escort to the boat' or 'to embark' (*sic* B.d.Cent.), as in Acts 17¹⁴ *'exapesteilan heōs epi tēn thalassan.'* This very natural gesture would not have been expressly mentioned. It must be assumed that the Corinthian delegates were to accompany the Apostle to Jerusalem, themselves conveying the sum which had been collected.[36]

1¹⁷ Here the writer defends himself against having made his decisions 'according to the flesh' (*'kata sarka bouleuomai'*), that is, following his personal desires and not according to the direction of the Spirit (a variant of the previous accusation). Again the defence is not very

---

[33] When had this promise been made? During a visit? Or in a letter? Perhaps in 13¹, if we agree that 10-13 were written before 1-9 (see Introduction).

[34] Even if we do not emend the *'charis'* to *'chara'* (with codex B) the word can signify 'joy', as Chrysostom has already urged, *MPG* 81, col. 408, and later BLEEK, *TSK* 1830, p. 622.

[35] If the visit related in Acts 18 is counted as the first, and the visit between the two extant Epistles as the second, then a third and fourth visit would be in question.

[36] WINDISCH perhaps considered this interpretation ('the Corinthian escort').— On the importance of the collection see M. GOGUEL, *RHPR* 1925, pp. 301-18, especially p. 302; the collection may imply a recognition of the supremacy of the Jerusalem Church. One could go further and suppose that it took the place of the tax sent to the Temple.

(18) [*No!*] *God is my guarantor that when we address you we do not utter an ambiguous ' Yes and No.'* (19) *For the Son of God, Jesus Christ, preached among you by us—by myself and Silvanus and Timothy—was no blend of ' Yes and No,' He was the very embodiment of the affirmation [of the truth].* (20) *He brought confirmation to all God's promises, and it is also through Him that we say ' So be it,' to the glory of God.*

convincing. For if, at that time, the journey had been in conformity with the divine will why had it not taken place? Nevertheless, the Corinthians must have conceded that the Apostle acted in good faith.

The end of v. 17 is difficult and controversial. It is more understandable if we depart from Nestlé and read with p 46, the Vulgate, and Bengel, and in conformity with v. 18: '*hina ē par' emoi to nai kai to ou*' = 'so that[37] (a consequence of 'fleshly' projects) I (Paul) say "Yes" and "No" at the same time' thereby affording proof of duplicity (Vulgate: '*ut sit apud me est et non*').[38] But why, with the majority of textual witnesses, are the 'yes' and the 'no' repeated ('*ou ou*' and '*nai nai*')? Did the Apostle wish to recall the word of Jesus reported in Matthew 5[37] ('let your word be Yes, yes; No, no')? Yet to begin with it is questionable whether Paul knew the saying, and furthermore it is not positively certain that Matthew has reported it correctly. The primitive form of this logion is perhaps recorded in the Epistle of James (5[12]): 'let your Yes be a yes, and your No be a no.' But this is precisely what the Apostle's opponents were unable to reproach him for. One is tempted to emend, with Markland and Barrington, to: '*hina ē par' emoi to nai ou kai to ou nai*' = 'so that my Yes means a No, and my No a Yes.'[39] This would be a well-stated accusation of duplicity. Yet since this is a purely conjectural reading we prefer that of p 46 and the Vulgate ('Yes and No'). The doubling of the 'Yes' and the 'No' might then be explained as a relatively late attempt to harmonise this text with that of St Matthew's Gospel. Verses 18 and 19, as we have indicated, appropriately read 'Yes and no,' which should be sufficient to settle the matter.

1[18]-20 God Himself is guarantor—that is the generally agreed meaning of '*pistos ho theos*,' and there are no grounds for departing from it

---

[37] In fact the '*hina*' here has consecutive force. This is no isolated case in N.T. language; see in particular Revelation 2[13] and John 9[2]: '*tis hēmarten hina tuphlos gennēthē*' ('who has sinned so that he should be born blind?').—Cf. BLASS–DEBRUNNER, § 391, and J. H. MOULTON, *A Grammar of N.T. Greek* I, p. 210.

[38] In addition, there was perhaps also the desire to insinuate that Paul possessed one of those weak consciences which was unable to decide between a 'yes' and a 'no', like that of King Epimetheus, according to K. SPITTELER (*Prometheus und Epimetheus*, 1920, p. 265f).

[39] Included in the collection of W. BOWYER: *Critical conjectures and observations on the N.T., collected from various authors*, 3rd edn, London 1782, p. 351.

(21) *Now it is God who has established us in Christ, along with you, and who has anointed us; (22) and it is He also who has marked us with His seal and has poured into our hearts the guarantee [of salvation], that is, the Holy Spirit. (23) For my part, I invoke God as witness against my very life, that it was to spare you that I did not come again to Corinth. (24) It is not that we wish to domineer over your faith; on the contrary, we are helpers of your joy. For you stand firm in the matter of faith.*

(Hebrew: *'ha'el hanne'eman'*).[40] For it is His Son who is preached by Paul, as also by Sosthenes[41] and Timothy. And there is no duplicity with the Christ. He does not say 'Yes and No'; His word is certain and final. He is 'the Yes', or, if we prefer it, 'Yes is the reply made through Him,' or, 'the Yes has become a reality in Him' (*'nai en autō gegonen'*).[42] The divine promises have been confirmed and achieved through Him (*'en autō to nai'* = 'in Him is the Yes'), and it is by faith that we can reply 'so be it'.[43] This 'Amen', prepared for by *'pistos'* = *'ne'eman'*, is quite in place here, and Revelation 22[20] seems to prove that it was customary to end prayers with this affirmation,[44] which here expresses an engagement on the part of the Christians to believe the promises.

The end of v. 20 is equally difficult. What is meant by 'to God for His glory through us' (*'to amēn tō theō pros doxan di' hēmōn'*)? Plummer translates 'through the faith of us.'[45] But it is perhaps rather a question of the witness which we render to the glory of God by making the pledge of faithfulness expressed by 'Amen'.

1[21–22] The opening phrase of these verses can be construed in two ways. Either we interpret it as: 'He who establishes us is God, and it is He also who . . .', or as 'God who has established us . . . is also He who . . .'. In either case it is necessary to supply an *'estin'* = 'is', which is lacking.   evertheless, we cannot escape the impression that the phrase is inco plete and that it should end with a benediction

[40] For *'pistos'* cf. *TWNT* vol. 6, p. 204 with the notes, as well as the text of Deuteronomy 7[9]: *'Theos ho pistos ho phulassōn tēn diathēkēn.'* Other texts in UNNIK, 'Reisepläne und Amen-Sagen, Zusammenhang und Gedankenfolge in 2 Kor. 1[15–25],' in *Studia Paulina in honorem Johannis de Zwaan*, Haarlem 1953, pp. 221ff.

[41] Concerning Sosthenes cf. our commentary on *The First Epistle of Saint Paul to the Corinthians*, ET 1961 (on 1 Corinthians 1[1]).

[42] Cf. Revelation 3[14]—No trace of 'dialectic' in Him, oh! Kierkegaard.

[43] Luther: 'Evermore strengthen our faith, so that we say the goodly Amen' (last verse of the Canticle 'Vater Unser im Himmelreich').

[44] In the O.T. 'Amen' is frequent as a community response, e.g. Deuteronomy 27[15–26]; Nehemiah 8[6]; Psalm 106[48]. In addition, it should be noticed how far the verses 18–20 which we are examining approach the Johannine idea of Christ as the one who witnesses to the truth of God (see especially John 5[36]).

[45] P. 30.

'may the God who ... bless you', then the omission of the *'estin'* would be explained.[46]

It is undeniable that the Trinity—God, the Son, the Holy Spirit—is mentioned here, though in a less classical way than at the end of the Epistle. But it is naturally the Pauline Trinity, which as yet knows nothing of the theology of the Councils,[47] and which is notably unaware of the personality of the Holy Spirit.—Do the terms *'chrisas'* and *'sphragisamenos'* = 'anointed' and 'sealed', allude to the diverse charismatic endowments of Christians, or do the participles in both cases (or in one or the other) have a reference to baptism? We think they refer to the gifts granted by the Holy Spirit. For as John Chrysostom had already observed,[48] it is not absolutely necessary to think of baptism, as Windisch, Lietzmann and Allo propose.[49]

'Ton arrhabōna tou pneumatos' ought not to be translated 'the earnest of the Spirit' as if it were a partitive genitive. In fact Pauline eschatology regarded in its totality shows that the Spirit is an instalment and guarantee of full salvation. So the genitive is explanatory or epexegetic, as in **5**[5], and it is in the same sense that the *'aparchē tou pneumatos'* is spoken of elsewhere (Romans 8[23]; cf. *'arrhabōn tēs klēronomias'*, i.e. the Spirit is 'an instalment of the inheritance,' Ephesians 1[14], and, for the heart of the matter, Hebrews 6[5]—Christians now already taste the power of the Spirit).

1[23] The Apostle now reveals the true motive in the changing of his travel plans. If he did not come to Corinth, then it was in order to spare the Church members, that is, so as not to cause them sadness yet once more (cf. **2**[1]). To add more weight to his statement he not only calls God to witness but pledges his very self (*'epi tēn emēn psuchēn'* = *'al-napšiy'*; *'hē emē psuchē'* is a way of saying 'myself'[50]). It is almost a conditional curse which he pronounces against himself (Windisch: *'Selbstverwünschung'*). We can see how near to his heart was the matter of re-establishing his integrity.

1[24] is a brief digression. The decision to spare the Corinthians is part of his constant concern not to appear as a tyrant or dictator (*'ouch*

---

[46] *'Bebaios'* also translates the root ' *'mn'*, cf. UNNIK, op. cit., p. 227. For the meaning of *'bebaioun'* and its connection with *'pistos'* and *'pistis'* cf. 1 Corinthians 1[6-8] and Colossians 2[7].

[47] Cf. F. MÉNÉGOZ, 'Trinité', *RHPR* 1938, pp. 448ff. On pre-Christian trinities v. *infra* 13[13].

[48] CHRYSOSTOM, *MPG* vol. 61, col. 411: 'What is anointing and sealing? The giving of the Spirit' (*'ti de esti, chrisas kai sphragisamenos; to pneuma dous'*).

[49] It is possible that the Jews had already used *'sphragis'* to denote circumcision (cf. Rom 4[11]). But of course that would not prove that the Apostle had considered baptism as replacing circumcision; and even if that were the case there is no necessity for him to think of baptism every time he used the word 'seal'.—The texts from the prophets and the Pseudepigrapha, cited by Windisch (p. 72) in this connection, teach us absolutely nothing.

[50] GESENIUS' Hebrew Lexicon, under *npš* 5.

hoti kurieoumen') who wanted to domineer over their faith, but as a servant having the duty of helping them to attain Christian joy (cf. 1 Cor 7³⁵).

CHAPTER II

(1) But I determined to myself not to cause you sadness a second time. (2) For if I make you sad, who then will make me glad? Certainly not the one who has been plunged into sorrow by me! (3) This is precisely why I wrote to you, to avoid being made sorrowful, at my visit, by those who ought to make me rejoice. For I have confidence in you all and I am sure that my joy is shared by you all.

2[1] *'Elthein en'* is an imitation of the Aramaic' *"'ata' b^e"* = 'to come with' which has the force of 'to cause', 'to bring'.[1] Therefore *'elthein in lupē'* = 'to cause sadness'. It was the sadness of the Corinthians which the Apostle Paul did not wish to aggravate by a fresh visit, since the cause of the whole unhappy situation (2[5ff] below) had still not at that time been removed.

2[2] is difficult. The *'kai'* in front of the *'tis'*, which the majority of scholars are happy to leave untranslated, must have the sense of 'then'.[2] But the meaning of the whole phrase remains somewhat obscure, not in the matter of grammar but of content. Giving such punctuation as does Nestlé (no stop between *'me'* and *'ei'*) it would be necessary to translate 'who could make me glad except the person to whom I cause sorrow'—a bizarre notion. We propose dividing the sentence into two, putting a question mark after *'me'*, and translating *'ei mē'* as 'certainly not.' The phrase then becomes intelligible: 'who would console me? Certainly not the one to whom. . . .' There is a hint of sarcasm in suggesting a fear of aggravating the malaise.

2[3] *'Egrapsa'* is not an epistolary aorist here, but a true aorist. The Apostle is referring to an earlier letter. So we come to a mention of the famous letter written 'in tears' (Sorrowful Letter).[3] *'Auto touto'* = 'precisely that'? But if Paul had already given in his letters an explanation of his motive in cancelling his journey, why does he solemnly repeat it? Perhaps because in this connection the letter had not made the desired impression. But an adverbial sense is also possible: 'precisely for that.'[4] This interpretation could be objected to on

---

[1] Cf. in particular Mark 8[38] par. (*'elthein en tē doxē'*).
[2] Cf. BLASS–DEBRUNNER §442, 9. 'Who then indeed?'
[3] Cf. Introduction.
[4] As 2 Peter 1[5]. Cf. Plato, *Protagoras* 2, p. 310 E.

(4) *It was, in fact, in profound sorrow and distress of heart that I wrote to you, shedding tears; not in order to grieve you, but to let you know the overwhelming affection I feel toward you.* (5) *And if somebody has given me an occasion for sorrow, it is not to me alone but to you all—let me say, to some extent, so as not to exaggerate.* (6) *The penalty meted out to him by the majority is sufficient punishment for the man.* (7) *On the contrary, it would be better now [as things are] that you forgive and console the unhappy man, so that he is not overwhelmed by excess of grief.* (8) *This is why I urge you to exercise love towards him.*

the ground that the adverbial force of the phrase is not certain when the verb does not have an object. But *'tēn epistolēn'* = 'the letter' can perfectly well be assumed.

Another aspect of the matter is now raised: Paul might have risked being grieved anew himself (*'lupēn schein'* = 'feel sad'). However, as the end of 2³ assumes, the Apostle's sadness is also that of the Corinthians.

2⁴ insists on the emotional distress of the writer at that time. *'Sunochē'* = 'anguish' or 'distress of heart.' The juxtaposition of *'sunochē'* and *'thlipsis'* recalls the *'thlipsis kai stenochōria'* of Romans 2⁹ (with the same meaning), as well as the *'anangkē kai thlipsis'* of 1 Thessalonians 3⁷.⁵

In 2⁴ᵇ Paul renews the assurance of his affection, as if he were afraid that the sadness of his letter may, in its turn, have grieved the Corinthians, although it was animated by the highest sentiments (*'agapē'* = 'love').

2⁵ gives us at last some indication of the root cause of the unhappy situation. Someone (*'tis'*, *'ho toioutos'*) had caused profound grief to the Apostle. Contrary to what Ch. Bruston thinks, it can scarcely be the incestuous person referred to in 1 Corinthians 5¹⁻⁵, for that incident was too long ago and had been settled by an anathema. It we wish to make an hypothesis, we can only suppose that the individual in question (*'ho toioutos'*)⁶ had attacked Paul's apostolate in a particularly insulting and offensive way.⁷ The revulsion could thus be felt as an insult to the entire community founded by the preaching of Paul. 'He has offended us all—at least [Paul adds] to some extent,' a limitation he adds in order not to exaggerate (*'epibarein'* = 'to be burdensome,' 'to put a burden on' someone).

2⁶⁻⁸ We gather from this that—doubtless as a sequel to the famous letter—the situation was cleared up and settled, the *'pleiones'*, i.e.

---

⁵ Cf. Psalm 106³⁹ and Psalm 24¹⁷ (LXX).

⁶ *'Toioutos'* not only denotes the person yonder, but a person of such a sort, 'this individual' (Loisy) or 'this unhappy person' (Osty). Compare also, perhaps, Philemon 9, *'toioutos hōs.'*

⁷ We understand better the irritation and the sadness of the Apostle, if his whole work had been put into question.

(9) *For in writing to you, my aim was to discover your attitude
by the test of your complete obedience.* (10) *Whoever you forgive,
I forgive also: and for my part, if indeed I have forgiven anything,
it has been for your sake and in the presence of Christ,* (11) *so that we
may not be Satan's dupes. For we are not ignorant of his intentions.*

the 'majority', or simply the congregation as such,[8] admitting that
the Apostle was in the right. Some penalty or punishment had been
inflicted by the congregation on the defaulter. What was it? Mere
disapproval, or exclusion from the community? The second possibility seems the more likely, since it would fully justify the exhortation
to forgiveness in 2[7]. The time has now come to exercise love towards
him, so that he will not be overwhelmed by distress. This clearly presupposes that he was penitent. '*Kuroō*' = 'to make valid,' 'to put
into practice.' '*Agapē*' does not necessarily allude to his re-admission
to the Agapé (*sic* Daechsel),[9] although forgiveness ought to have this
effect.

2[9] is a little surprising. Paul had stated that he did not wish to intervene other than discreetly; nevertheless, he has wished to put the
Church to the test ('*dokimē*' = 'the attitude in testing'), in order to
see whether they would be obedient up to the hilt. However, it would
seem that this submission of a Christian ('*hupakoē*') is always basically a submission to Christ. So it is, in short, a matter of testing their
piety and their wisdom, and not merely their obedience to the
Apostle, even though he would be able to demand it, in such cases,
by appealing to his apostolic status.

2[10] '*Charizomai*' = 'to grant' a favour, a kindness, or *forgiveness.* If
the Apostle grants forgiveness, it is in the interest of the Church, and
he takes the responsibility in the name of Christ. '*Ei ti kecharismai*' =
'if, indeed, I have forgiven anything' introduces a qualification hard
to explain. Doubtless it is implied or recalled that the Church had
already taken the initiative in this forgiveness, and the Apostle can
only confirm it.

2[11] '*Pleonektein*' has here the meaning, as frequently, of taking by
trickery, 'to deceive.' '*Ouk agnooumen*' = 'we are not ignorant
...' could be a slogan borrowed from the Gnostics, who sometimes

---

[8] '*Pleiones*' probably means the same as '*hoi polloi*', Romans 5[15,19], viz. 'the
community,' 'the whole group.'
[9] TH. DAECHSEL, *Paulus, der Apostel Jesu Christi,* Dresden 1913 (cited by
WINDISCH, p. 89).

(12) *Now, on arriving at Troas, to preach there the good news of Christ, I found a door opened by the Lord.* (13) *Yet I had no rest in spirit, because I did not find my brother Titus there. So after having said farewell to them* [*the Christians*]*, I departed for Macedonia.*

boasted of knowing the deep things of Satan.[10] Paul is also aware of the need to put the Church members on guard against his devices and in particular his attempts to divide the Church, which might be facilitated by the complete exclusion of this defaulter. Happy are they who are alert to his 'machinations' (Calvin) and can frustrate them! Unfortunate the folk who know them not (or who do not even any longer believe in his existence), for this puts them in the position of not being able to defend themselves![11]

2[12f] The Apostle starts to outline the journey which he made, not to Corinth but to Macedonia. It is useless to try to discover it in the Acts of the Apostles, for the book is far too fragmentary.—'*Trōas*' is not the province but the seaport, the precise name for which was '*Alexandreia Trōas.*' Here one embarked for Macedonia (Acts 16[8–11]). The Apostle stayed there at the time of his first journey into Greece, and halted there later before going to Jerusalem (Acts 20[5–6]); cf. the certainly historically genuine reference in 2 Timothy 4[13] about things left at Troas.—'*Thura aneōgmenē*' = 'a door wide open.' As Windisch observes, the expression could, in the first place, have a merely prosaic sense, namely, that of finding a lodging and a room for discussions as well as for preaching, in circumstances where the synagogue may have been closed against him. But it is its religious meaning which is of primary importance: hearts were opened to the Gospel, and the Apostle must have felt some distress at abandoning this congregation prematurely. The farewell he took of them ('*apotaxamenos*') would not have been expressly mentioned if it had not had a rather solemn character.

The reason for this departure is given in 2[12,13]. Titus, whom the Apostle had been disappointed not to find at Troas (where he should have met him), had still not arrived. His absence disquieted Paul.

'*Ouk eschēka anesin*' = 'I found no rest' (Calvin: 'relief'). He adds: '*to pneumati mou*' = 'in my spirit' or rather 'for my spirit.' '*Tō mē heurein me*' = 'because I failed to find' (it seems to be a matter of an infinitive construction with dative of the cause, which is nothing unusual).—Titus, whose name does not occur in Acts, is mentioned again in Galatians 2[1,3] as having once accompanied Paul to Jerusalem, and in 2 Timothy 4[10] as staying (preaching?) at some time or other in Dalmatia. According to the Epistle addressed to him, he may

[10] Cf. the article on the Devil in the *Vocabulary of the Bible*, ET London 1958, and Revelation 2[24]: 'know . . . the deep things of Satan, as they say.'
[11] 'Satan's greatest trick is to create the belief that he does not exist' (a saying attributed to Jean-Frédéric Oberlin).

(14) *But thanks be to God, who always associates us with His triumph in Christ and who diffuses through us in every place the odour of knowledge about Himself.* (15) *For we are the fragrance of Christ to the glory of God, among those who are going towards salvation and among those who go to their destruction.* (16) *I mean that for the latter we are a deadly fume which leads to death, but to the former an odour of life which leads towards life.—And who is equipped for this? [We are.]* (17) *For we do not go hawking the word of God as if it were trash, in the way others do. But it is in a spirit free from self-interest, and conscious that the word comes from God, that we preach as members of Christ and in the sight of God.*

later on have played an important part in the organisation of the Churches of Crete; and the reference to this can retain its value even if the Epistle is pseudepigraphic. By birth he was a Gentile, but Paul, in conformity with his principles, did not have him circumcised (Gal 2³).—The Apostle abruptly interrupts the narrative of his journey, to re-continue it only at 7⁵. It is as though we were at the edge of a ditch, and a wide one at that, with the other side visible at 7⁵. 7⁵ joins with a very nice fit to 2¹³ (rather like the drifted continents in Wegener's hypothesis). It is understandable that some scholars have regarded 2¹⁴–7⁴ as a separate letter, inserted here by error. But the hypothesis can be dispensed with. We can suppose that after a break in the dictating, Paul may have felt the need to open his heart fully and to return later to the subject, after being reminded of it by Timothy; or, again, we may simply suppose that 2¹²,¹³ are not in place, but originally occurred just before 7⁵, from whence they were by some error detached. The good linkage between 2¹⁴ and 2¹¹ strengthens this view: after having spoken of the wiles of Satan, the writer glorifies God who has frustrated them.

2¹⁴⁻¹⁷ '*Thriambeuō tina*' normally means 'to triumph over someone,' a meaning unacceptable here, where it is a matter of God triumphing through Christ ('*en tō Christō*') over visible enemies; and the Apostle is involved, not, of course, as one of the vanquished, but like a victorious general.[12]

'*Osmē tēs gnōseōs*' = 'odour of knowledge' is an expression which has not been coined by our author. It is found already in the Wisdom literature (cf. Ecclus 24¹⁵; 39¹⁴, as well as the Syriac Apoc. of Baruch 67⁶). But there is a curious development in the use of the

---

[12] In the same way the god Dionysus associates his votaries with his royal progress. The lexicons of Estienne and of Bauer admit this sense of '*thriambeuein*' with the accusative. It is a sort of hiphil. WILLIAMS renders: 'God leads us in his triumph.'

metaphor.[13] For in 2^{15} the Apostle himself is the fragrance of Christ ('*euōdia Christou*').

But this perfume is not always experienced in its proper nature; there are those upon whom it has a disastrous effect—those, namely, who reject the Gospel, and for whom it is a 'stench of death' ('*osmē tou thanatou*', 2^{16}). This 'stench' leads unbelievers to their death ('*eis thanaton*', 2^{16}). For those who, on the other hand, accept Christianity, the Apostle radiates an odour of life, which leads to life ('*ek zōēs eis zōēn*'). For a similar contrast between the contrary impact of the same given reality we can compare 1 Corinthians $1^{18,23,24}$, where the preaching of the cross is a cause of stumbling to some and a source of new life to others.[14]

Notice the use of the present tense '*sōzomenoi*'. To the Apostle neither salvation nor perdition are completed facts; the participles used denote 'men on the way to salvation,' or on the way to perdition (see also 1 Cor 1^{18}).

The end of 2^{16} has a question without an answer: 'Who is qualified for these things?' i.e. for preaching the Gospel. The implied answer is: We are—'and we do not distort the word of God as so many do.'

The verb '*kapēleuō*' already with Plato (and much later with Philostratus) has the sense of 'adulterating a truth' or 'making merchandise' of it.[15] Bengel: 'hucksters adulterate . . . they act for profit.' '*Kapēloi*' = 'hucksters' are in fact people who sell shoddy goods. This

---

[13] Cf. E. LOHMEYER: 'Vom göttlichen Wohlgeruch', *Sitzungsberichte der Heidelberger Akademie*, 1919, *Philologisch-historische Klasse*, bk 9. Sometimes Genesis Rabba 34, on Genesis 8^{21} is quoted, where Abraham is said to radiate a pleasant odour (FREEDMANN, p. 273). But if we trouble to read the context it is to be seen that this is quite a special case: Abraham was one day thrown into a fiery furnace and his flesh, lightly singed by the flames, gave off an exquisite fragrance. According to Zohar 74a (ed. J. de Pauly, Paris 1906 ff, vol. 5, p. 210) Israel gives forth a pleasant odour when it has in its numbers a high proportion of righteous. —In the Mandaean literature the Saviour communicates fragrance to the prisoners he has delivered:'and they became sweet-smelling by my perfume' (Left Ginza, Ch. 24, LIDZBARSKI, p. 549).

[14] Certain mystics have asserted that the love of God causes the wicked to suffer and that this is the true source of the pains of hell.—According to some Rabbis, the Torah, likewise, can give either life or death, cf. Talmud Bab. Yoma, 72b (GOLDSCHMIDT II, p. 966). —On the subject of our passage also cf. T. W. MANSON, '2 Corinthians 2^{14-17}', suggestions towards an exegesis,' in *Studia Paulina in honorem Johannis de Zwaan*, Haarlem 1953, pp. 155ff., cf. STUMPFF, '*euōdia*', in *TWNT* II, p. 808.

[15] Cf. Plato, *Protagoras*, 5, p. 313 C.: '*ho sophistēs tungchanei ōn emporos tis ē kapēlos tōn agōgimōn*,' the sophist is a merchant or retail-dealer in knowledge. Philostratus, *Life of Apollonius*: '*sophian kapēleuein*' = 'to hawk wisdom around' (Teubner edn, vol. 1, 16, p. 13).—F. PRAT, *La théologie de saint Paul*, 1949, I, p. 173, mentions texts in which innkeepers who adulterate wine are called '*kapēleuontes*'. According to DAVIES (p. 133) travelling Jewish merchants sometimes made proselytes.

is why it is necessary to possess integrity ('eilikrinia') for the preaching of the word, i.e. to be free from self-seeking motives. Always it must be remembered that truth comes from God ('*ek theou*') and that we bear before God ('*katenanti theou*') the responsibility for its faithful transmission.

'*Hoi polloi*' has a pejorative force here as with the Greek philosophers; it means the mob of evil preachers, i.e. false apostles, the predecessors of those mentioned in the 'Teaching of the Twelve Apostles'.[16] Many good texts, however, amongst them p 46 and D, read '*hoi loipoi*' = 'the others'. '*Hōs*' (cf. $2^{17b, 17c}$) does not have comparative or restricting force ('as if'), but a qualificatory sense: one must preach in so far as one is conscious of the responsibility of the task.[17] It is a sign of the rapid expansion of Christianity that there were already so many counterfeit preachers of the Pauline Gospel.[18]

At all events, the transition from v. 16 to v. 17 is not very clear. There is an ellipse, and the words 'we are; for . . .' must be understood.

[16] *Didache*, Ch. 11.
[17] BEATUS HISPANUS (*MSL* 96, col. 932) says: '*Sicut ex Deo loquitur et non coram Deo.*' He therefore seems to imply a text which read '*ou katenanti*'. Nevertheless, he had previously quoted the text in its usual form, but this quotation may have been corrected by a copyist or editor.
[18] Concerning 'false prophets' see below, 10^{12ff}; 11^{16ff}.

CHAPTER III

(1) *Are we starting again recommending ourselves to you? Or do we need, like some other people, letters of commendation to present to you, or from your hand?* (2) *Our letter consists of you yourselves, a letter written in your hearts, read and recognised by all the world.* (3) *For you are obviously a letter of Christ's written through our efforts. It was not written in ink, but by the Spirit of the living God, nor engraven on tablets of stone, but upon hearts of flesh.* (4) *We have this assurance through Christ in the sight of God.*

3¹ Why '*palin*' = 'again'? It could in fact be an allusion to 1 Corinthians 9ff, or indeed to the letter of four chapters (**10–13**), if, as we think, this preceded **1–9**. Letters of recommendation ('*sustatikai epistolai*') could have been written by other Churches to be presented at Corinth, or the other way round. But Paul has no need of any ('*mē chrēzomen*'). However, the use of such letters seems to have been already widespread and was indeed justifiable in view of the false prophets who abused the confidence of the Churches—though unfortunately it did not prevent even these being recommended here and there.[1] What matters to Paul is the mission which God has entrusted to him and the work which he must accomplish for Him. It is this which he will explain in what follows, from **3⁴** onwards.

3²⁻³ Here the writer takes up and develops an idea previously touched upon in 1 Corinthians 9², where, however, the metaphor is different. His letter of commendation is here the Church itself. Of this letter he says: (a) that it is written in our hearts ('*en tais kardias hēmōn*') or in your hearts;[2] (b) that it is read by every one, which is a hyperbolic way of saying 'by all who have opportunity to read it.' '*Ginōskomenē kai anaginōskomenē*' is a play on words difficult to keep in translation—perhaps 'read and recognised.' (c) This letter bears the stamp of authenticity on itself, for the Corinthians themselves demonstrate ('*phaneroumenoi*' is middle voice) that they are the letter. (d) It is Christ's letter, which in a sense He has dictated. (e) It has been written (or delivered) 'by us' ('*diakonētheisa huph' hēmōn*'). (f) It was not written with ink ('*to melan*' = 'black ink', usually made with soot), but with the Spirit of the Living God ('*tō pneumati tou theo zōntos*'). (g) Unlike the Law of the Old Covenant, the letter was not written on

---

[1] 'Have you ever met a bad shepherd who was not recommended by some sheep farmer or other?' a wise old man once asked me.
[2] '*Hēmōn*' according to the commonly accepted text. The reading '*humōn*', though poorly attested (S and 33), agrees better with the context and we prefer it.

(5) *Not that we are capable, of ourselves, to put anything to our credit; for our qualification comes from God. (6) He it is who has empowered us to be the servants of a new covenant, not of the letter, but of the Spirit. For the letter kills, but the Spirit gives life. (7) Now if the ministry of death, engraven letter by letter on tablets of stone appeared surrounded by such brilliant glory that the children of Israel could not fix their gaze upon Moses' face because of its glory (although it was only transient), (8) how much more glorious will be the ministry of the Spirit! (9) For if the ministry of condemnation was glorious, how much more is it true that the ministry of righteousness abounds in glory. (10) So that which has been partially glorified has, in the last analysis, not been glorified at all, compared with the superabundant splendour [of the new administration]. (11) For if the transient ministry had its time of glory, by how much more is the enduring ministration glorious!*

tablets of stone, but, in agreement with the prediction of Jeremiah 31³³ (LXX 38³¹), on men's hearts, and stress is laid on the fact that it is on hearts of flesh and not on stone—which again is an allusion to this great prophetic word and a good example of the use of the Old Testament.

3⁴⁻¹¹ contrast the ministry of Christ and His Apostles to that of Moses.

3⁴ *'Pepoithēsis'* has here almost the same meaning as *'parrhēsia'* in Hebrews 10¹⁹, i.e. 'courage' to approach God and to appear before Him.

3⁵ If Paul is aware of any ability for his work it is not from any native endowment (*'aph' heautōn'*) but because God Himself has enabled him (*'hikanotēs ek tou theou'*). The term *'logisasthai'* deserves a brief comment. We should not translate (with B. de Cent., Strachan) 'qualified to form any judgement' or even (with Loisy) 'manage something for ourselves'. It is better to retain the basic meaning of 'attribute to someone'; the Apostle's abilities must not be regard as his natural endowments. The infinitive has here final force (= in order that), though a consecutive force is not excluded (= so that).³

3⁶⁻¹¹ This passage, as Auguste Sabatier said, is dominated by the opposition between the religion of authority and the religion of the spirit. The former leads to death; the latter, to life. The former enjoys only passing prestige; the second, an eternal glory. To some extent the Apostle is inspired by the famous words of Jeremiah already

---

³ Cf. note 37, p. 10.

quoted, which foretold of a time when the hearts of men would be changed and would no longer be hearts of stone. These predictions, according to the Apostle Paul, were fulfilled when the Holy Spirit was granted to believers.—For the meaning of '*diathēkē*' see the Bibliography and the discussion in our Commentary on the Epistle to the Hebrews,[4] and also the *Vocabulary of the Bible*.[5] Almost always '*diathēkē*' means 'covenant' and nothing else. Yet in v. 14 we translate '*palaia diathēkē*' as 'Old Testament,' because it refers to the books we always speak of in that way.

The opposition between letter ('*gramma*') and spirit ('*pneuma*') signifies in the first place the opposition between the written Law and the law of the Spirit. Then it describes two ways of reading the Law of Moses: a literal way of reading it (cf. '*epōrōthē*' v. 14) and a spiritual way. To this extent the Apostle is in perfect agreement with Philo. But whilst, for the Alexandrine Rabbi, the key to Scriptural interpretation is given by a kind of theosophy, Paul sees in Christ the one who removes the veil of Moses. This is a kind of symbolic representation of the way in which the Rabbis read the Law, for in their case a veil still covers the Scriptures, or, more precisely, their understanding (cf. v. 15). '*Noēmata*' (v. 14) and '*kardia*' (v. 15) are both synonyms for 'thoughts'.

The acknowledgement of this does not contradict the spiritual character of the Law. For, as John Chrysostom stresses,[6] the Law does not supply the Spirit ('*pneuma ou pareichen*'), which alone can penetrate its profound meaning and can give life; it is clearly not the Law but sin, he adds, which produces death. Nevertheless, the Law understood in an external and legalistic way does not prevent men from fulfilling their natural destiny, which is to go 'to the devil.' It is also known how far devotion to the letter encourages Pharisaism, that is, the tendency to expect salvation by works.[7]

Along with the opposition between legalism and spiritualism is associated that between the Jewish ministry and the Christian apostolate (3[7–11]). The former is seen as an administration of condemnation because, as it does not bring salvation, it leads to damnation ('*diakonia tēs katakriseōs*' v. 9). The latter is called a '*diakonia tēs*

---

[4] Commentaire du Nouveau Testament vol. xii, *L'épître aux Hébreux*, Delachaux and Niestlé, 1954, ET in preparation.

[5] ET London 1958.

[6] Cf. 'Homélie I ad II Cor.' *MSW* 61, col. 438ff.—For a study of the developments in Romans on this point, we refer to F. J. LEENHARDT's commentary (ET London 1961), to the two-volume commentary of OLTRAMARE (1881–2), to DODD (Moffatt Commentaries), to NYGREN (ET 1952) and to OTTO MICHEL (in the Meyer Kommentar 1954).

[7] The opposition between 'spirit' and 'letter' extends, in fact, beyond the realm of religion. How often in the history of philosophy one finds that disciples have become untrue to their master's teaching through clinging to the letter of his teaching!

(12) *Having therefore such a hope we are full of confidence,* (13) *and we do not act as Moses did, who put a veil over his face (so that the people of Israel could not perceive the ultimate significance of that which was to be abolished).* (14) *But their minds became hardened [and that is why] the same veil remains drawn, even today [in spite of everything], at the reading of the Old Testament.*

dikaiosunēs' = 'ministry of righteousness' (v. 9) because it leads those who believe to the righteousness which comes from God.[8]

Furthermore, the Jewish administration was only transient (as v. 10 implies, but v. 13 says expressly), while the second was eternal (*'eis to menon'*). This may seem a surprising remark for a writer to make who believes in the imminent end of the world, but he is obviously thinking chiefly of the administration of Christ of which the ministry of the Apostles is a kind of (unsurpassable) earthly manifestation.[9]

Even the first administration also had its period of 'glory'; this became visible when the face of Moses on Sinai was illuminated (or surrounded) by a splendour which the eyes of the Israelites could not bear to look upon.[10] How much more splendid must be the 'glory' of the Christian administration! And this assertion should not only suggest the honour which is due to it, but also the 'glorious' state destined for believers when the Lord returns 'with glory.'

3[7] *'Tupoō'* = 'to engrave in.' *'Egenēthē in doxē'* = 'appeared in glory,' 'had its moment of glory,' when the face of Moses was so illumined that the Israelites were unable to gaze upon it (*'atenizo'* as Acts 3[4]). Yet that glory was destined to disappear (which is the force of *'katargoumenē'*).[11] Concerning Moses' veil cf. Exodus 34[33-35].[12]

3[9] *'Perisseuō'* must mean 'to abound'. If the verb were merely used to express the comparative (be still greater than) it would be redundant with *'mallon'*.

---

[8] Cf. Romans 3–4 and the commentaries mentioned above.

[9] Here again the Epistle to the Hebrews gives a detailed and original commentary on this Pauline idea.—The eternal priesthood of which Paul speaks is precisely that of Melchizedek, which is the central theme of that Epistle.

[10] Rabbinic texts about the 'glory' of Moses are naturally not lacking, but they give hardly any information of value for the exegesis of this passage. Cf. STRACK–BILLERBECK, III, p. 113f.

[11] Once more a present participle denotes something which is to happen, as *'sōzomenoi'* or *'apollumenoi'*. Do not render: 'the last rays of that glory,' as though it had disappeared. Osty gives the good translation: 'the glory which was but transient.'

[12] Some historians of religion have thought that Moses wore a cultic mask. The typology would not suffer if this were so, since the sense of the Bible has in some degree been 'masked' in the past. Cf. GRESSMANN, 'Moses und seine Zeit,' *Forschungen zur Religion und Literatur des A. und N.T.*, Neue Folge, I, 1913, pp. 246–51.

(15) *But until today, every time that Moses is read, a veil lies over their minds. It cannot be removed, because it is only through Christ that it is abolished.* (16) *When Israel is converted, the veil is stripped away.* (17) *For there where the Lord is, is the Spirit; and where the Spirit is, is the liberty of the Lord.* (18) *We all reflect the glory of the Lord with faces uncovered, and are transformed into His image, from glory to glory; for this takes place through the Spirit of the Lord.*

3^{10} '*En toutō tō merei*' (Vulg.: '*in hac parte*') is difficult, and many scholars are happy not to translate these words. The restriction must be supposed to belong to the second '*dedoxasmenon*'. Thus the entire phrase means: that which has been glorified within limits (i.e. the transient and limited character of the old administration) has not really been glorified at all with respect to the (new) superabundant glory.[13] '*Heneken*' = 'on account of.'—3^{11} summarizes 3^{7-10}

3^{12} '*Chrēsthai*' is used like the Latin '*uti*'.

3^{13-16} A verb is to be supplied in v. 13 between '*ou*' and '*kathaper*': 'we do not act as Moses did who. . . .'[14]—'*Atenisai eis to telos*' = 'to look upon the end' (the splendour) of what must vanish away? As though the Israelites should not be present at its disappearance? But in that case the Apostle would have contradicted himself, because a totally different motive is suggested in v. 7. Then can '*telos*' really mean the final radiation of the glory which is unbearable even to the last? *Sic* Strachan. But the Jewish ministration was only just beginning. The Vulgate has '*in faciem*', implying the reading '*eis to prosōpon*,' which is ill-attested in Greek.[15] A final solution to the difficulty would seem to be suggested by the well-known phrase of Romans 10^4: '*telos gar nomou Christos*' = 'Christ is the end of the Law' when 'end' ('*telos*') means 'goal' or 'ultimate significance.'[16] Now the Israelites would be able to see this sense; for the Apostle speaks without any reserve (v. 12). But ('*alla*' v. 14) their understanding was blocked ('*epōrōthē*'). It is necessary first that they should be converted (v. 16),

---

[13] It is perhaps surprising that the writer did not compare Moses' glory with that of the transfiguration of Jesus. Though the omission is no proof of the legendary nature of the latter narrative.

[14] BLASS–DEBRUNNER, § 482: 'we do not do. . . .'

[15] Almost only by A.

[16] '*Telos*' can also mean 'the full development of,' 'the consummation of' (cf. Plato, *Symposium* 210E and 211B). This would give a good enough sense to our text, though such a meaning for '*telos*' seems not to occur in the Bible except perhaps in James 5^{11}. For '*telos*' = 'aim' cf. also 1 Timothy 1^5.—H. J. SCHOEPS, 'Paulus als rabbinischer Exeget,' in his book *Aus frühchristlicher Zeit*, 1950, quotes Jewish texts announcing the end of the Torah in the World to Come (pp. 224ff). For Paul, this future age was already present, a claim which can be supported. —LUTHER (Erlangen edn, vol. 64, p. 234 on 2 Corinthians 3^{15-18}) contrasts the veiled face of Moses and the unveiled face of the Lord.

for Christ is the only one who can remove the veil (v. 14b).[17] According to Nestlé this was predicted in Exodus 34[34] (apparently quoted in 3[16]), a passage which speaks of conversion to God ('*pros kurion*'), but in which the Apostle may have identified Christ with '*kurios*', as he very often does. Such exegesis may seem forced, yet fundamentally it is reasonable, for the prophecy is fulfilled in Christianity which aims at the true conversion, if not of Israel 'after the flesh', then at least of those who are spiritual people.

3[17-18] draws the conclusions of the affirmation about the removal of the veil, and gives classic expression to the new conditions of Christian existence and above all of its spiritual freedom, together with the transformation into the image of Christ.

3[17] contains one serious difficulty to which scholars do not always pay sufficient attention. Christ seems to be identified with the Holy Spirit, and this presupposes a personification of the Spirit in complete variance with Pauline pneumatology, in which the Spirit is very carefully distinguished from God and from Christ (see also 13[13]). Hence we cannot follow Lietzmann, who thinks that Paul regards the Spirit and Christ as essentially one and the same ('the Messiah . . . in reality the Spirit itself,' p. 1). On the contrary we agree with Plummer and Allo in their judgement that the personal identity of the two cannot be intended here. But while Plummer nevertheless concludes hesitantly 'we must be content to remain in doubt' (p. 104), Allo, following F. Prat[18] takes 'spirit' not to be the Holy Spirit but simply the 'spirit' which is opposed to the 'letter' in 3[6]. Then Christ would be, in a sense, the principle by which the Scriptures are correctly understood. Such a 'spirit' would neither be identical with God nor Christ.

Yet there is a matter of style which prompts us towards a more speculative explanation. 3[17b] reads '*hou de to pneuma kuriou, eleutheria*' = 'there where the Spirit of the Lord is, is liberty,' or, as we

---

[17] In 3[13] why '*mē atenisai*' and not '*ouk*'? Because the infinitive preceding the '*eis to*', having basically purposive force, has retained its preference for '*mē*', even when taking a consecutive sense as here. Other instances of the consecutive usage are: Romans 12[2]; 2 Corinthians 8[6]; Galatians 3[17]. Even subordinate clauses introduced by '*hina*' sometimes have consecutive force (1 Jn 1[9]; Rev 13[13]). Conversely, '*hōste*' can express purpose, cf. Luke 20[20]; Matthew 27[1] (cf. MOULTON vol. I, p. 207). S. CASTELLION, *Biblia Sacra Latina*, 1551, interprets 3[14b] as follows: the Jews have not discovered that the veil is only removed by Christ. Certainly '*hoti*' can mean 'that'; but it would be curious if '*anakaluptomenon*' had the above meaning; moreover this participle should then be preceded by '*autois*'. Yet BACHMANN still explains the verse in a similar way: 'without it being thereby disclosed that in Christ it is done away.' Likewise G. GODET.

[18] *La théologie de saint Paul*, 1949, vol. II, pp. 525ff.

would prefer to punctuate: *'hou de to pneuma, kuriou eleutheria'* = 'there where the Spirit is, is the liberty of the Lord.' Now, as v. 17b clearly constitutes something of a distich with v. 17a, one is tempted to follow Graverol[19] and to read v. 17a as *'hou de ho kurios, to pneuma estin'* = 'there where the Lord is, is the Spirit.' Then one obtains perfect parallelism both of style and thought between the two members. This is why we yield to the temptation of accepting this conjecture, although there is no textual evidence to support it.

If we displace the comma in v. 17b and put it between *'pneuma'* and *'kuriou'* the reason is that it is not simply any sort of freedom which is in question, but that which comes from the Lord. How the Apostle had had to struggle against the confusion between Christian liberty and fleshly licence! Christian freedom definitely involves also freedom from the bondage of corruption, freedom from fear (fear of death, fear of life), as well as freedom from ourselves (and from the complexes to which some are enslaved).

3[18] reaffirms that for us the glory is no longer veiled; yet why is it apparently said that we contemplate it only as in a mirror (*'katoptrizomenoi'* v. 18, cf. 1 Cor 13[12] *'di' esoptrou'*)?[20] Because we make the mistake of taking the participle as in middle voice, whereas in fact it is passive (we act as a mirror), that means that we 'reflect' the glory in question. This awe-inspiring prospect[21] has a further consequence, though one, it is true, for which we have already been prepared by the famous passage in 1 Corinthians 15[49]—believers are destined to be 'transformed' (*'meta-morphoumenoi'*) 'according to the same image,'[22] *'tēn autēn eikona,'* i.e. the image of the Lord (*'kuriou'*, at the beginning of the verse). *'Apo doxēs'* = 'from glory', 'by glory,' indicating the

---

[19] Graverol (an Anglican priest), in an extract from a letter published by JEAN JÉRÉMIE LE CLERC (died 1736) in his *Bibliothèque Universelle* (Amsterdam 1686 ff.), vol. IX, p. 203. The conjecture was adopted by Markland (cf. W. Bowyer, *Critical conjectures and observations on the N.T.*, collected from various authors, 3rd edn, London 1782, p. 352). Markland even claimed to have found the reading in the ms.f, though this is unhappily not confirmed by Scrivener's edition of F (Cambridge 1859).—PIERSON and NABER, *Verisimilia*, 1886, p. 121, cut the knot by suppressing v. 17 as an interpolation.

For contemporary Catholic exegesis of this verse consult PRÜMM, 'Die katholische Auslegung 2 Kor. 3. 17a in den letzten vier Jahrzehnten,' *Biblica*, 1950, pp. 316–45, 459–82, and 1951, pp. 1–24.—Schneider's monograph, 'Dominus autem Spiritus' (Rome, Officium Libri Catholici), mentioned in *RB* 1952, p. 129, was not available to us.—Cf. also the literature cited by DAVIES, p. 196, note 1.

[20] Cf. N. HUGEDÉ, *La métaphore du miroir dans les épîtres de saint Paul aux Corinthiens*, Neuchâtel and Paris 1957.

[21] Every Christian has become a Moses, and yet his glory is superior to Moses'.

[22] It could also be translated: 'to become the same image,' the accusative would then denote the result of the transformation. BLASS–DEBRUNNER, § 159 (4): 'into the same form.'

S.E.C.—4

source; '*eis doxan*' = 'for' or 'towards glory,' the result of the transformation. Bearing in mind the whole of the Apostle's teaching (cf. notably Rom 8 and 1 Cor 15), it must be admitted that this transformation takes place here below in the unseen (inward) man, the nucleus of the new creature, to be manifested only at the time of the resurrection.

At the end of the verse '*kathaper*' has causative, not comparative or restrictive force. It is definitely the Spirit of the Lord ('*apo kuriou pneumatos*') which produces this change.[23]

[23] '*Kathaper*' or '*kathōsper*' can in fact be so used. See the lexicons.

CHAPTER IV

(1) *Here is the reason why, being entrusted with this ministry by the mercy [of God], we do not lose courage.* (2) *We have repudiated the shameful intrigues that are hatched in secret. Neither do we behave like knaves, falsifying the word of God; on the contrary, by making the truth known openly, we commend ourselves to every human conscience, in the sight of God.* (3) *And even if our Gospel is veiled, it is so only among those who are perishing,* (4) *that is among unbelievers, whose mind the god of this age has blinded to prevent them from contemplating the splendour of the Gospel of the glory of Christ, who is the image of God.* (5) *It is not ourselves we are proclaiming, but Jesus Christ the Lord. We ourselves are merely your slaves for Jesus' sake.*

In the light of the truths previously outlined, **4** characterises the Apostle's ministry, with the dominant feature a paradoxical polarity, namely the tension between the sublimity of his mission and the misery of his outward existence.

4$^{1-2}$ '*Kathōs*' = 'according as' or 'in compliance with,' showing that the source of his ministry goes back to God's gracious mercy.[1] '*Engkakoō*' = 'to grow lax,' 'to lose courage.' '*Apolegesthai*' (here the aorist '*apeipametha*' for '*apeipometha*') is a technical term for expressing the rejection or abandonment of a belief or practice. What the writer is rejecting is the '*krupta tēs aischunēs*,' i.e. 'underhand dealings' of which one should be ashamed; the genitive is a genitive of quality. The B.d.Cent. renders: 'the intrigues that are hatched in secret.' The sequel shows that the Apostle is not merely defending himself against suspicions of this kind, but is passing to the offensive by accusing the 'false prophets' of dishonesty. '*Panourgia*' is something worse than guile or malice; it is the behaviour of a person who is equal to doing anything (cf. **12**^{16}). '*Dolountes ton logon tou theou*' = 'falsifying the Gospel message (the theology),' i.e. 'giving adulterated teaching' (cf. **2**^{17}). The Apostle, for his part, commends himself ('*sunistanō*', as in **3**^{1}) by the truth he teaches, which bears its own hallmark, at least in the eyes of all men who have moral and religious awareness ('*suneidēsin enōpion tou theou*').[2]

4$^{3-4}$ cause us to reproach Paul with a measure of obscurity. Windisch even supposes that there were some esoteric truths which Paul was

---

[1] The passive of '*eleeō*' in the sense of 'find mercy' is attested in Matthew 5^7.
[2] If '*anthrōpoi*' also includes pagans, this supports the assertion of Romans 1 and 2, where the Apostle attributes to them also a minimum of moral awareness and (in principle) of religious intuition.

obliged to hide, but nothing of the kind is suggested by what follows. The Apostle adds that it is the reprobate alone ('those on the way to perdition' = '*hoi apollumenoi*,' 2^{15})[3] who grasp nothing of this; these are they who refuse to believe ('*apistoi*') and whose minds have been blinded by the 'god of this world' ('*ho theos tou aiōnos toutou*'), i.e. the Devil.[4]

The construction of 4^4 is syntactically shocking, because the dative '*hois*' is continued by the genitive '*tōn apistōn*'; and '*ta noēmata tōn apistōn*' must not be translated 'their unbelieving minds,' because '*apistōn*' is preceded by the article. The meaning must be (unless it is a matter of a simple slip): in such folk it can be seen that the god of this world is in the habit of blinding the thoughts of unbelievers; at all events, it is to be noted that it is the devil and not God who makes them unperceptive.

'*Augazō*' (or '*kataugazō*', or again, according to some texts, '*diaugazō*') = 'to see clearly,' 'to contemplate.' The meaning 'to reflect' would also be very acceptable having regard to 3^{18}, but it is ill-attested.[5]

The accumulation of genitives ('*tou euanggeliou tēs doxēs tou Christou*') is so pleonastic, and the reference to the Gospel equally superfluous, that one is driven to assume that '*tou euanggeliou*' (or '*tou Christou*'?) is a gloss.

The end of v. 4 alludes to one of the strangest features of Pauline Christology—that already, in His pre-existent state, Christ is the perfect image of God, cf. 1 Corinthians 11^7; Colossians 1^{15}.[6] That is why he is also the heavenly man, i.e. the perfect man. We have seen that empirical man is destined to exemplify ultimately the image of Christ (1 Cor 15^{49}; 3^{18}) and hence to return to a state of being 'in the image of God' (Gen 2^{28}, cf. 1 Cor 11^7).

4^5 The writer often calls himself the 'servant' or 'slave' of Christ (Rom

---

[3] Perhaps this is too sweeping an assertion, for the author of the Second Epistle attributed to Peter also found obscurities in the Pauline letters, as have other good Christians since his time (cf. 2 Pet $3^{15,16}$).—'*En tois apollumenois*' and '*en hois*' are taken to be neuter by J. A. BAIN, ET 1918, pp. 380ff; and P. H. HÖPFL, *ibid.* pp. 428ff, thinks that Eusebius and Erasmus were of the same opinion. This would ease the grammar of 4^4. But we have been unable, in the last resort, to convince ourselves that it would yield a better sense.

[4] This is the only N.T. passage in which Satan is called a god. Certainly, in St John's Gospel he is called 'the ruler of this world' ('*archōn tou aiōnos toutou*'). It is needless to add that there is never any question of a metaphysical dualism like the Mazdaean (which the Essenes perhaps took up). The devil is always a creature, as are the 'gods' referred to in 1 Corinthians 8^5.

[5] '*Augazō*' (and its compounds), used with the accusative, can mean 'to enlighten.' But this sense is not relevant here.

[6] The idea is the same in Philippians 2^6, where '*morphē*' is synonymous with '*eikōn*'. On this matter see our article 'Kyrios Anthropos,' *RHPR* 1936, pp. 196–209.

(6) *For it is God who has said 'Let light spring forth from the darkness,' which light has shone also in our hearts, in order to give us the
illuminating knowledge of the glory of God in the face of Christ.* (7) *But
we carry this treasure in earthen vessels, so that it can be seen that its
incomparable power comes from God and does not have its origin in us.*
(8) [*Thus,*] *we are hemmed in on every side, yet not crushed; perplexed, but not despairing;* (9) *pursued, but not overtaken; overwhelmed,
but not annihilated,* (10) *carrying always and everywhere in our body the
mortification of Jesus, so that Jesus' life may likewise be evident in our
body.* (11) *In fact, we who have this life, are nevertheless always being
committed to death in our mortal bodies for Jesus' sake,* (12) *so that
death is at work in us, but life in you.*

1^1; Gal 1^{10}; Phil 1^1; cf. Tit 1^1). Here he goes a step further. He is also
the servant of the Corinthians for Jesus' sake.[7]

4^6 is very important, but difficult. In the first place, the construction
is incorrect: a main verb is lacking. The text might be clarified by removing the '*hos*',[8] and this would then make '*elampsen*' (= 'has
shined'?) the verb we need. Or '*estin*' might be inserted, either after
'*theos*' (i.e. 'God it is who said,' &c.) or before '*hos*' (i.e. 'God who
said ... is also He who', &c.). But the principal difficulty is of a
theological kind. The usual rendering according to which 'God has
shined in our hearts' ('*hos elampsen en tais kardiais hēmōn*') implies an
utter theological misconception. For the idea that God the Father
can be or become immanent in man in order to enlighten him is an
inconceivable notion in the context of Pauline thought. Bachmann,
who has accurately sensed the difficulty, gets round it by giving
'*elampsen*' transitive force (as the Hebrew hiphil): 'God has caused
His light to shine in our hearts'; but unfortunately the object is lacking. There is only one way of keeping this interpretation, and that is
to emend '*hos*' to '*ho*'. One can then translate: 'and it is this light
which ("*ho*") God has caused to shine in our hearts.' In that case the
normal intransitive force of the verb can just as well be retained, with
the translation: 'for it is God who has said "Let light shine forth out
of darkness," which light ("*ho*") has shone also in our hearts.'[10]
    Since the writer uses the plural not only for the pronoun ('*hēmōn*'),
but also for the noun 'hearts' ('*kardiai*'), the statement must not be
taken in too personal a way; Christians in general[11] are meant, as in

---

[7] With Nestlé, we prefer the reading '*dia Iesoun.*' '*Dia Iesou,*' although sup
ported by p 46 and S, is on the whole less well attested and does not give so good
a sense.

[8] A text without '*hos*' is given by D, G and certain other witnesses.

[9] '*Lampō*' is indeed attested in secular Greek literature in the transitive,
Bachmann truly discerns. Cf., e.g., Euripides, *Helen* 1131: '*dolion astera lampsas*'
he (Nauplius) lit a deceptive beacon (i.e. to make the Greek fleet run aground).

[10] Is it possible that Paul (or Timothy) may have made a slip by taking '*phōs*' as
a masculine noun, as is the noun of the same spelling '*phōs*' = 'man'?

[11] That would exclude right away a reference to the Damascus road experience,
which, moreover, never involved any 'inner' light.

2 Peter 1[19] where all Christians are promised that the *'phōsphoros'* ('the morning star,' Christ, and not God) shall arise in their hearts.

As the light God kindles has no need to be 'enlightened', *'phōtismos'* must have the active meaning of 'light', 'illumination', as in 4[4] and Psalm 26 (27)[1].—*'Tēs gnōseōs'* is an explanatory genitive: the light which illumines us is 'the knowledge,' i.e. the knowledge of the glory (*'tēs doxēs'*—genitive of the object) of God, shining from the face of Christ (*'en prosōpō Christou'*).[12]

4[7] Even in antiquity earthen vessels or pots (*'ostrakina skeuē'*) were symbols of weakness.[13] The comparison is well chosen, because it is the feeble body which the spirit of the Christian inhabits—and in particular that of the Apostle—the very feebleness of which 'according to the flesh' is once again teleologically justified by the necessity for revealing his overflowing energy (*'huperbolē tēs dunameōs'*) as a gift of God's grace; cf. 1 Corinthians 1[26ff].

But the celebrated antitheses of 4[8-9], with their unique optimistic pessimism, add one important feature: even in the outward events of an eventful life Providence has always preserved his life from the worst. For the meaning of the participles, see the translation we give, following that of Osty. All that need be added is that *'exaporoumenoi'* (lit. 'in a situation with no outlet') is a rare verb, occurring in the Bible only in Psalm 87[16] (LXX); 1[8]; and here. But the meaning is clear: it describes the situation of someone who is at his wits' end (*'ex'*), i.e. in a desperate plight. *'Ouk engkataleipomenoi'* may be rendered 'not forsaken,' i.e. by God; and this, if I am not mistaken, is how all the translations take it. But we may imagine that the writer, continuing the metaphor of the race (*'diōkō'* = 'to pursue') wanted to imply that he never remained at the rear.

4[10] seems to re-open the eschatological perspective: the Apostle shares in the death of Christ through his own sufferings (*'nekrōsis'* = 'mortification'), which kill the old Adam so that the new Adam may emerge. But 4[11,12] show that he is also thinking of an actual manifestation of this new life, and thinking of it in two ways. On the one hand, God has preserved him from utter disaster, so that the new life is manifest by his mere physical existence (*'en tō sōmati hēmōn'*); and, on the other, he is a bearer of life to others. This idea is strikingly and concisely expressed in 4[12]. Death is at work in us, but life in you —and between these two is the relation of cause and effect. The more

---

[12] Here, again, there is no occasion to attribute to *'prosōpon'* the unusual meaning of 'person'. What is meant is the face or the 'figure' of Christ (in a 'figurative' sense).

[13] Cf. Aesop's familiar fable of the earthenware jar and the iron pot (edn 'Les Belles Lettres,' Paris 1927), which La Fontaine takes up, though altering the meaning. However, in order to prove that a most unprepossessing Rabbi could be a source of great wisdom reference was sometimes made to the usefulness of earthen vessels for storing good wine. Cf. STRACK–BILLERBECK I, p. 861.

(13) *Having the same spirit which inspired the Scripture passage:
'I believed, therefore I spoke,' we also believe, and this is why we
speak.* (14) *For we know that He who raised up the Lord Jesus will
raise us also in communion with Him, and will present us with you
[in God's presence].* (15) *All these events, indeed, have taken place
for your sakes, so that the grace generously spreading amongst
the multitude [of Christians] may make thanksgiving also abound,
to the glory of God.* (16) *This is why we do not lose courage. On
the contrary, even if our outward man is destroyed, our inward man,
in return, is renewed day by day.* (17) *For the present light affliction
produces for us a weight of glory, abundant and unfailing in eternity,*
(18) *on condition that we do not fix our gaze upon the visible world, but
towards the world unseen. For the visible world is transitory, but the
unseen world is eternal.*

the Apostle suffers, the more his life flows out upon the Corinthians
(cf. 1^{4-7}!). As for details: '*thanatos*', as in 1^{10}, means 'danger of death,'
and doubtless also the 'domination (or ascendancy) of death;'
'*periphero*' is lit. 'to carry around,' i.e. on his missionary journeys;
'*sarx*' and '*soma*' seem to be used here without distinction for 'body'
or 'bodily existence.'

4^{13-15} Even if in this present world their roles seem to be divided—
'death' for the Apostle, 'life' for his congregation—there will be no
difference in the world of the resurrection. All will participate in that
—both we (*hemas*') and you ('*sun humin*')—and all will in some way
be in the retinue of Christ, without whom our new life and our resurrection would be but vain imaginings (1 Cor 15). The expression '*sun
Iesou egerei*' = 'God will raise us up with Jesus,' excludes the idea of
a resurrection in the past, whether with Christ or at baptism, which
nevertheless are suggested in Colossians 3^1 ('you have been raised
with Christ') and Colossians 2^{12} ('you have been raised in Him').[14]
—As P. Bonnard remarks in his valuable study 'Dying and living with
Christ',[15] the phrase '*sun Christo*' = 'with Christ' has been much
less studied than '*en Christo*' = 'in Christ.' At least we must observe
that the former has several meanings for Paul which must be
distinguished.[16] Here, as we have said, '*sun Christo*' emphasises that
Christians will share in the company of Christ.

4^{13b} gives a quotation from Psalm 115^1 (116^{10}), introduced by '*kata
to gegrammenon*' = 'according to Scripture.' As in the Psalmist's

---

[14] This fact appears to us to confirm an earlier date for the Epistle to the
Colossians than for 2 Corinthians and Romans, wherein the Apostle avoids these
forms of expression which must have caused some misunderstandings.
[15] *RHPR* 1956, pp. 101–12.
[16] Thus H. J. Schoeps, *Aus frühchristlicher Zeit*, 1950, p. 294, who wants to
explain the phrase solely by the *imitatio Christi* motif, seems to be regarding it in
a very one-sided way.

case, faith is a necessary condition for the proclamation of the truth. Is it also the sufficient condition? In other places the Spirit is also judged to be necessary. But these two gifts of grace are inseparable.[17]

If we neglect the context, 4^{16-18} could have been written by Philo (or another Platonist). As with him, the invisible world, regarded as perfect and permanent, is distinguished from the visible; while the opposition between an outward and inner man is even reminiscent of Hermetic terminology. Nevertheless, if we take into account the whole of the Apostle's teaching, we are in fact compelled to regard the passage from the eschatological angle, a viewpoint unacceptable to Platonists and Hermeticists. What is the inner man (*'ho esō hēmōn'* scil. *'anthrōpos'*), if not the new Adam, who grows mysteriously until the time of his 'revelation' (Rom 8^{19})?[18] *'Ta mē blepomena'* = 'what we do not see,' could in principle be equivalent to *'ta aorata'* (Col 1^{16}), denoting the created worlds we cannot perceive (the worlds of angels). But as in Romans 8^{24-25} 'what we do not see' is regarded as an object of hope, it is better to take it as the new aeon, which will be eternal (*'aiōnia'*, v. 18). 4^{18} reminds us again, indeed, about our tribulations, that the glory (*'doxa'*)—key concept of the resurrection world—is in a measure engendered (*'katergazomai* = lit. 'to produce') by the present affliction (*'thlipsis'*) which is transitory (*'parautika'*). These tribulations are a small matter (*'elaphron'*) in comparison with the 'weight of glory' (*'baros doxēs'*) which will be unfailing in eternity (*'aiōnion'*). The expression *'kath' huperbolēn eis huperbolēn'* = lit. 'in a superabundant way and giving abundance,' seems somewhat pleonastic. Doubtless *'kath' huperbolēn'* is to denote the process and *'eis huperbolēn'* the result of this mysterious increase of the sum of glory.[19]

Why *'mē skopountōn hēmōn'* and not *'ouk'*? Because the conditional

----

[17] *'Ta panta'* = 'all things,' in 4^{15}, does not seem to have its usual significance of 'the universe,' but the entire divine dispensation, which aims at the salvation of those who have faith, and the gift of the Holy Spirit (*'charis'*) in particular. This grace will manifest itself abundantly in the Christian community and will give rise to an outburst of thanksgiving (*'tēn eucharistian perisseusē'*) to the glory of God. In what way? Certainly not in words alone. Possibly this remark is already a discreet announcement of the result of the collection at Corinth. *'Perisseuō'* as a transitive is rare, but it is attested amongst other instances by 9^{8a} and Matthew 13^{12} par.

[18] The preposition *'ana'* in the compound verb *'anakainoun'* must not induce us to regard the 'inner man' as an entity existing prior to conversion and merely purified thereby. He appertains to the new creation, and, in spite of the tribulations of the outward man (the old Adam within us), continually receives new power and courage. However, the other sense of *'ana'* as 'upwards' seems actually to be perceptible here. The well-known verse Psalm 102 (103)[5] *'anakainō-thēsetai hē neotēs sou'* ('your youth is renewed') clearly does not have the same meaning, although this does not mean that the Psalmist had not glimpsed a larger truth.

[19] 'Having been disciplined a little, they (the righteous) will receive great good,' Wisdom 3^5; cf. Romans 8^{18}!

force of 'if we do not fix our attention on what is visible, but' is still felt. Once again we learn that, for the Apostle, salvation is not a magical or automatic process.[20]

[20] To preachers eager for modern metaphors we might suggest the slogan: the way of salvation is no escalator.

CHAPTER V

(1) *For we know that when our earthly house, which is a mere tent, is destroyed, we have a dwelling that comes from God, an eternal house in heaven, made by no human hand.* (2) *And so we sigh in this present house, while longing to be clothed by the heavenly body which will be our dwelling;* (3) *so that having been clothed by it we may not be found naked.* (4) *In fact, we who are in this tent groan under our burden; for we do not wish to be unclothed but to be re-clothed, so that what is mortal is swallowed up by life.* (5) *And He who has fixed this destiny for us is God, who has given us the Spirit as guarantee.*

5[1-10] is one of the best known and most striking passages of this Epistle. The Apostle rises above his obsession of not being able to complete his task, by the serene acceptance of two alternatives— either to continue his work here below or be reunited with the Lord.

5[1] '*Oidamen*' = 'we know,' introduces a traditional notion which, in itself, is no new revelation. Apocalyptic already spoke of new 'dwelling-places' reserved for the faithful in the future Age.[1] Yet the Apostle gives new meaning to this 'future house' ('*oikia*', '*oikodomē*'). Like '*skēnos*' = 'tent', both terms denote the human body. Here below we dwell in an 'earthly tent,' which is our fleshly body ('*oikia tou skēnous*' —the genitive being explanatory): our house is our tent. After it is taken down ('*kataluthē*'), we are sure of having a house which is not made with 'human hands,' i.e. by human begetting,[2] but which comes from God ('*ek theou*') and which is found 'in heaven' ('*en tois ouranois*'). These details put the finishing touches to Paul's teaching on the new man. We know that while existing in embryo here below among believers who belong to the body of Christ, it (the new man) does not yet have a visible individual body. This body already exists elsewhere, viz. 'in heaven.'

5[2-4] is rather difficult. Certainly, we understand why we 'sigh' ('*stenazomen*') in this body, which Romans 7[24] is going to call a 'body

---

[1] See John 14[2]; cf. Slavonic Enoch 61[1]: 'In the great Age [to come] are many mansions prepared for men, good for the good, and bad for the bad . . . Blessed are those who enter the good houses.'—With St Paul the concept is slightly different; those who are rejected have no dwelling-places at all.

[2] This way of speaking—a contrast between the tent made by human hands and the heavenly mansion—is somewhat reminiscent of that used in the Epistle to the Hebrews (Chs 8 and 9) and by Philo, to contrast the Jewish tabernacle with the heavenly sanctuary. For Philo cf. *Quaestiones in Genesin I. 28 ad Gen. 2. 23* (ET of the Armenian text by Ralph Marcus, London and Cambridge, Mass., pp. 16–17, which appeared as a supplement to the Loeb *Classical Library* edition of Philo).

(6) *We are always full of courage, therefore, although we know that domiciled in this body we are exiled from the presence of the Lord* (7) (*for we walk by faith, not by sight*). (8) *We are therefore full of courage and we would prefer to be exiled from our body and domiciled near to the Lord.* (9) *Yet our ambition is to please him, whether we have our dwelling near to Him or are exiled away from Him.* (10) *For we must all be brought to the light before Christ's tribunal, so that each may receive the fruits of what he has accomplished by using the possibilities of his bodily life, whether for good or ill.*

of death' (not merely because it will die, but also because it carries death within itself), and which here is compared with a burden ('*baroumenoi*').[3] But what is the meaning of '*ependusasthai*' = 'to put on over' (G. Godet)? It is necessary clearly to observe the alternatives envisaged by the Apostle. On the one hand, he may be alive at the time of the parousia, in which case he will put on the glorious body over the earthly body ('*ependusasthai*'), which will, in a sense, be swallowed up by it, as, in general, death will be swallowed up by life ('*katapothē hupo tēs zōēs*,' v. 4). 1 Corinthians 15[53–55] is an excellent commentary on this passage, even though the term '*ependusasthai*' does not occur in it.[4]

The other possibility—which he does not desire ('*ou thelomen*')—is to lose the earthly body, that is, to die before the parousia and thus before being able to be clothed by the new body. He would then be 'found naked' ('gumnoi', v. 3), a possibility he views with aversion,[5] and which is exactly what will be avoided if he can be clothed

On the other hand, tent ('*skēnōma*') with the same meaning as here of body is also found in 2 Peter 1[13]. Cf. also the expression '*skēnoun*' in John 1[14], which means 'take up dwelling in a tent.'—For the O.T., cf. in Job 4[19] the pessimistic way in which the earthly body is spoken of, as a house of clay, as dust. Cf. Wisdom 9[15]: 'a perishable body weighs down the soul.'

According to T. W. MANSON, *JTS* 1945, pp. 1–10, and DAVIES (p. 313), the term '*skēnos*' might, in the last analysis, have been suggested by the Feast of Tabernacles (cf. Mk 9[5]!), which is plausible.

[3] Is it necessary to reiterate that this visible corporeal existence is no evil in itself, as it is for Platonists who call the body a tomb ('*sōma*' = '*sēma*')? What follows shows that the Apostle's attitude is entirely different.

[4] The idea of splendid celestial clothing kept for the holy is a concept of apocalyptic, found also in Matthew 17[2] (transfiguration).—Glorious heavenly garments are also a favourite subject in Mandaean literature; cf. the Left Ginza, Chapter 60 (LIDZBARSKY, p. 593): 'I put upon him the clothing of the great Life . . . I hastened to put on him the clothing of living fire, I took him up and set him up in the house of perfection ("*Vollendung*").' Cf. also the Left Ginza, Chapters 19, 35, 49, 50, 51; cf. similarly the Odes of Solomon 25.8: 'I was overlaid with the covering of thy spirit.'

For Slavonic Enoch, cf. Ch. 9 (p. 25 in the edition of Vaillant). For Paul's concept of a spiritual body, see H. CLAVIER, 'Brèves remarques sur la notion de "*sōma pneumatikon*",' *The Background of the New Testament and its Eschatology. In honour of C. H. Dodd,* Cambridge 1956, pp. 342–62.

[5] The ideal of a purely immaterial existence, so dear to Platonists, Gnostics and Kantians, is therefore at the opposite pole to the Pauline eschatology and feeling. On this point we will agree completely with G. SEVENSTER, 'Some remarks on the "*gumnos*" in 2 Cor. 5. 3,' *Studia Paulina in honorem J. de Zwaan,* Haarlem

with the glorious body before losing this one. That is the meaning
of the much-discussed ending of v. 3.[6]

Contrary to the opinion of many scholars, we therefore see no
doctrinal contradiction between 1 Corinthians 15 and 5. Never at
any time did the Apostle envisage taking possession of the glory-
body before the parousia. This is precisely why the state intermediate
between death and resurrection is characterised as 'nakedness'.
Nevertheless, the hope of the resurrection condition remains un-
shaken. 5[5] emphasises this. It is God who prepares us for this
glorious state ('*katergasamenos hēmas*'), and He has given us the
Holy Spirit as a guarantee (cf. Romans 8[23]; Ephesians 1[1]; Hebrews
6[5]).[7]

Having made this admission, it is all the more remarkable that in
what follows (5[6-10]) the Apostle, by his piety, is lifted to a spiritual
plane where even the fear of 'nakedness' affects him no more. He will
go so far as to prefer death, to be with his Lord.

However, to understand the text some details must be considered.

5[6] In every eventuality ('*pantote*') the Apostle preserves his trustful
courage ('*tharrountes*'); he takes up the alternatives elaborated in
5[3-4], but views them in a different spirit. If he continues in the body
('*endēmountes en tō sōmati*'), he is 'exiled' from the Lord ('*ekdē-
moumen apo tou kuriou*').[8]

5[7] reminds us that here below we cannot yet see the Lord; we continue to walk by faith ('*dia pisteōs peripatoumen*') and not by sight
('*dia eidous*'). Basically, it is the same affirmation as in 1 Corinthians
13[12], where the (future) knowledge is said to be 'face to face' ('*prosōpon pros prosōpon*');[9] cf. also Romans 8[24].

The other possibility (5[8]) is to be exiled from the body (i.e. from
every sort of body!), but to live near to the Lord ('*endēmēsai pros ton*

1953, pp. 202ff. We also think, as this author does, that Paul's view of survival
must not be equated too swiftly with the existence of a 'soul' or 'spirit'. Certainly,
as among the Jews, belief in a semi-material existence like that of the shades in
Hades, must be reckoned with. Hence 'nakedness' is only relative, though none-
theless resented as a privation.—The idea of the soul in popular Greek religion
was entirely analogous, as E. Rohde once proved in his study *Psyche*, ET London
1925.

[6] It matters little whether we read '*eiper*' in v. 3, with p 46, B, D, or '*ei ge*,' with
Nestlé and the other witnesses; in any case it is a hypothetical proposition because
the eventuality which Paul would prefer is not certain ('*endusasthai*' has here the
same meaning as '*ependusasthai*').

[7] For Rabbinic theology concerning resurrection (very complex and far from
homogeneous), see DAVIES, pp. 311–18.

[8] The grammatical construction of 5[6] is not in order; again, a finite verb is
lacking. Some witnesses (e.g. S) repeat '*tharrountes*' in v. 8 instead of reading
'*tharroumen*'. This would allow a stop to be placed prior to v. 8, and to regard v. 7
as a parenthesis, making '*eudokoumen*' the principal verb. It is a way of removing
the lack of grammatical sequence, and is moreover well attested.

[9] Cf. Numbers 12[8] where it is said of Moses that he speaks to God '*stoma kata
stoma*' (lit. 'mouth to mouth') and '*en eidei*' ('by' or 'in sight'). '*Eidei*' is then
synonymous with '*stoma kata stoma*'.

kurion'). Here the Apostle gives the preference to this second possibility (*'eudokoumen mallon'*), which implies a veritable reversal of values (nakedness preferable to the present life!)—though without putting in question the supreme worth of life with the Lord in a glorious body.

Taking up this attitude implies a fresh religious intuition of the greatest importance: the state intermediate between death and resurrection, at least for those who are united with Christ, in no degree involves the destruction of the personality; the latter will even enjoy the near presence of Christ, yet without possessing complete felicity.[10]

5^9 gives the final word of the practical solution to the dilemma of **5.**[8] While preferring to be present with the Lord, the Apostle submits to the divine will. He has no ambition (*'philotimoumetha'*) but that of being acceptable (*'euarestoi einai'*) to Christ, i.e. of fulfilling His commands, whether in this world or the next.[11]

It is to be remembered that an illuminating commentary on this passage is given in Philippians 1^{18-26}, which we cannot study in detail here.[12] The outlook is the same, only the Apostle adds that to continue his earthly life, although to be preferred less than existence with Christ, may be necessary for the sake of others (*'di' humas'*, Philippians 1^{24}).

Why does 5^{10} suddenly refer to the judgement? Because all believers will not have fulfilled their tasks with the same conscientiousness; they will not all be *'euarestoi'* = 'well-pleasing' (v. 9) to the same extent. As in 1 Corinthians 3, the judgement of Christians only is in mind.[13] Of course, the salvation they have obtained through faith is not put in any doubt. According to 1 Corinthians 3^{15}, even someone who has worked less well will be saved, though he will lose a reward (*'zēmiōthēsetai'*) to which others have a right. Thus a certain grading will take place in the future world, a grading by which believers— let us not fear the expression—will be judged according to their works. We do not know whether this judgement takes place immediately

[10] For the state of the Christian between death and resurrection, cf. Ph. Menoud, *Le sort des trépassés d'après le Nouveau Testament*, Neuchatel and Paris, 1945, as well as the conclusion to our article 'Eschatologie biblique et idéalisme platonicien' in *The Background of the New Testament, Essays presented to C. H. Dodd*, Cambridge 1956, pp. 444–63.

[11] It is possible to debate whether *'endēmountes'* in 5^9 means life in the body or life with the Lord (and *'ekdēmountes'* the reverse, respectively), but hardly to avoid seeing that it comes to the same thing in the end. For the meaning of *'areskō'* cf. our Commentary on 1 Corinthians *ad* 7^{32-3}.

[12] Cf. the excellent commentary by P. Bonnard: *L'épître de saint Paul aux Philippiens*, Delachaux et Niestlé, Neuchâtel 1950.

[13] As for unbelievers and apostates, their fate is determined in advance. They are destined to vanish. On this topic see our article 'Y a-t-il une double résurrection chez saint Paul?' *RHPR* 1932, pp. 300–20, and Allo, 'Saint Paul et la double résurrection corporelle, '*RB* 1932, vol. 41, pp. 187–209.

(11) *Knowing, therefore, what the fear of the Lord implies, we try to convince men, while in God's presence we ourselves are presented just as we are—as we hope we are to your consciences.*

after death or at the parousia. The Apostle makes no express pronouncement on the question.[14]

As for details: *'phanerōthēnai'* could be middle (= 'reveal himself') or passive (= 'be revealed'). The parallel text in 1 Corinthians 4[5] makes us opt for the passive. *'Bēma'* is the tribunal platform where the judge sits, and then the judge's seat; in some instances a 'throne' (cf. Rom 14[10]). 'We all' according to our interpretation means 'all Christians.'—The second half of the sentence is confused; the text is far from certain. If we translate the text Nestlé gives it will have to be thus: 'in order that each one may get the things [done] by means of his body (*"ta dia tou sōmatos"*) in proportion to what he has done (*"pros ha epraxen"*), whether good or evil (*"phaulon"*).' But the meaning of *'pros ha epraxen'* is doubtful. The construction *'ta dia tou sōmatos'* is equally unclear. P 46 reads *'ta idia'* = 'his own things,' instead of *'ta dia,'* which is interesting (and is the reading implied by the Latin witnesses[15]); but with this again the meaning of *'sōma'* (= 'life'?) is very strange. The passage reminds us of Revelation 14[12]. But here it is not a question, properly speaking, of works done, but of the rewards which follow them and which come to the doer. *'Phaulos'* = 'bad', as opposed to *'agathos'* = 'good', has no doubt been chosen deliberately. For *'kakos'* would imply an evil intention such as could not be attributed to the elect (any more than to a missionary working with unsuitable methods, 1 Cor 3[12f]). *'Phaulos'* is indicative, rather, of something of inferior quality, very ordinary, done without care, something worthless.[16] Windisch is surprised that the Apostle speaks only of actions which are black and white, taking no account of grey. But our interpretation of Paul's view of the judgement does not exclude a graded series.

The following passage (5[11]–6[13]) gives further information of the way the author conceives his apostolate and his relationship with his parishioners.

5[11] *'Eidotes'* = 'being fully conscious of.'—*'Peithō'* = 'to try to

[14] Extra-Pauline testimonies diverge. Matthew 25 puts the judgement at the last day. Luke 16[19], in the story of Lazarus and the Rich Man, gives things differently, cf. Hebrews 9[27]. It can be added that the Ezra Apocalypse, which teaches a final resurrection, nevertheless refers to the punishment of the wicked immediately after death (2 Esdras 7[75–101]).

[15] One reading which, among the Greek MSS, D alone supports reads *'ha dia tou sōmatos epraxen.'* This is doubtless an intelligent emendation of the text, but it is not the original reading. The Vulgate has: *'ut referat unusquisque propria corporis prout gessit sive bonum sive malum.'* This presupposes the reading *'ta idia tou sōmatos,'* &c. If a conjecture is allowable, we would like to read *'dia tou stomatos'* (for *'dia tou sōmatos'*): he shall receive 'from the mouth' (of the judge) a reward in conformity with his works.

[16] This is one more reason for avoiding the banal reading *'kakon'*, although it is supported by p 46, B, D and the Textus Receptus.

(12) *We do not want yet again to be 'putting ourselves forward.'
But we do not want to give you a motive for taking up our defence,
so that you may have something to answer to those who glory in
appearances and not in inward worth.* (13) *For when we are 'out of
our mind,' it is for God's sake; when we are 'of sound mind,' it is for
yours.* (14) *For love for Christ possesses us because we have reached the
conviction that he died for all. Yet (someone will say) all have died.*
(15) *True, but He has died for all, so that those who live should no more
live for themselves, but for Him who for their sake experienced death
and resurrection.*

persuade'—though not, of course, regardless of the means, as some
have perhaps reproached the Apostle of doing (cf. what follows). For
his thoughts and intentions are not hidden from God, the fear of
whom (*'phobos tou kuriou'*) does not leave him. *'Pephanerōmetha'*: the
perfect can have present meaning, 'we are visible just as we are.' In
v. 11b the Apostle hopes that the Corinthians are equally aware of
what he really is (literally: 'I hope that I am revealed also in your
consciences,' *'en tais suneidēsin humōn'*).

5¹² The Apostle, having the appearance of commending himself
(*'sunistanomen'*) yet again (*'palin'*), now opens a new theme: he wants
to put his recipients in the position (*'aphormēn didonai'* = 'to give an
opportunity') of taking up his defence (*'kauchēma'*) against his
adversaries, who are doubtless false apostles like those referred to in
4¹⁻² and below in **10¹²**, **11⁴, ¹²⁻¹⁴, ²⁰**. They are depicted as people who
derive their glory from appearances (*'en prosōpō kauchasthai'*), but
could not boast of their real intentions (*'en tē kardia'*).[17]

5¹³ This verse reveals implicitly a particular reproach hurled at the
Apostle of which we have not previously heard (at least, if we have not
studied previously the four chapters **10–13**). He is regarded as more
or less abnormal or mad.[18] Certainly the verb used (*'exestēmen'* =
lit. 'we are in ecstasy') could in principle be taken in a good sense;
but there is reason to give it here the same pejorative sense as in Mark
3²¹; cf. *'aphrona einai,'* **11¹¹**; 'All right,' Paul replies, 'but that concerns God only. So far as you are concerned, in my relations with
you I am of sober spirit' (*'sōphronoumen'*; G. Godet, 'of composed
mind').

5¹⁴⁻¹⁵ *'Sunechō'* = 'to keep together,' 'to contain,' 'to constrain.'—
In the expression *'agapē tou Christou'* = 'love of Christ,' the genitive

---

[17] Many witnesses read *'ouk'* for *'mē'*. in particular D, C, G and the Textus
Receptus. But, without being over-meticulous, the use of *'mē'* could be justified
from the underlying conditional element—they could not boast of what is in
their hearts, even if they wished.—*'En prosōpō kai mē en tē kardia'* might also be
rendered 'they boast before men but not in their own conscience.' But why not?

[18] 'The selection of this surprising alternative of *"ekstēnai"* and *"sophronein"*
was probably caused by the declaration of some of his opponents that he was not
only paradoxical and obscure (4³), but quite crazy,' PLUMMER, p. 172.

(16) *Consequently, from now onwards we know no one according to his fleshly being. And if we have known a Christ according to the flesh, we now know Him so no more.* (17) *So that if anyone is a new creature in Christ, the old order has passed, and, behold, a new world has arisen.* (18) *Now the author of all the worlds is God, and He it is who has reconciled us to Himself through Christ and has committed to us the ministry of reconciliation.*

could in principle be a subjective genitive, but with Spicq we regard it as a genitive of the object. Love for Christ is incoercible, because it is based upon the clear conviction that Christ died for us.[19] If it is objected (*'ara'*): yet all have died; the reply must be: yes, but nevertheless He died *for all*, and besides that is raised for all.[20] The implication is that we must no more live for ourselves (*'heautois'*), but for Him.

5[16] The transition from v. 15 to v. 16 is difficult. Why is the refusal to know anyone 'according to the flesh' (*'kata sarka'*) a consequence (*'hōste'*) of the preceding statements? No doubt because in addressing people who have been made anew no further account need be taken of the circumstances of the life of the old Adam (nor of sins committed prior to conversion). But the application of this principle to Christ creates new difficulties. What, in the first instance, is the precise meaning of *'ei kai'*, &c?[21] 'If we have known'? or 'even if we had known'?[22] It is difficult to decide; but in any case it is risky to find support in this verse either for asserting or denying that Paul had 'known' Jesus in His earthly life. What is certain is that 'the Jesus of history' (in modern parlance) only interested him in His main features: His humiliation (Phil 2), His death and resurrection—that is, precisely in those features which the Bultmann school regard as more or less mythical. It is the risen Christ and the place He occupies in the life of the Church and of its members which is the centre of his Christology. Clearly, one could ask, with F. C. Bauer,[23] Holsten, and some others, whether Christ *'kata sarka'* does not mean the Jewish political-messianic concept ('Christos' = 'anointed' = 'Messiah'). But we agree with Windisch, who thinks that such a matter is not even raised here. What is more likely is that yet again Paul is defending himself against those who will only admit Jesus' contemporary disciples as Apostles (see Plummer).

[19] C. SPICQ, 'L'étreinte de la charité,' *Studia Theologica*, VIII. 2, Lund 1954, pp. 123–32.
[20] Notice that *'krinein'*, like our 'decide', not only means to judge or reach a decision, but also to arrive at a conviction.
[21] Some witnesses read *'ei de kai'* or *'kai ei'*; this is of no importance.
[22] F. PRAT, *La théologie de saint Paul*, 1949, I, p. 28, comes down decisively for the hypothetical: 'even if we had known. . . .' We ourselves would be less decisive.
[23] F. C. BAUER, *Paulus, der Apostel Jesu Christi*, 1843, p. 288 (= 2nd edn I, p. 304), 'the "*Christos kata sarka*" is only the Christ or Messiah of Judaism'; cf. HOLSTEN, *Zum Evangelium des Paulus und Petrus*, Rostock 1868, pp. 69ff.

So we come to the famous v. 17, one of the most important of the Epistle: the old world ('*ta archaia*') has vanished away—a sublime anticipation, justified by the existence of the Church and of the new life, which are realities. This new life is even called a 'new creation,'[24] because the new Adam belongs already to the new world. But what is the relation between v. 17a and v. 17b? With the Vulgate and with Bachmann, our view is that the comma should be placed, not after '*Christō*' but after '*ktisis*': 'if anyone is a new creature in Christ, then —for him—the old order has passed and a new world has arisen ("*gegonen*").' Expectation of a new world is common in Christianity, but the assertion just made is of a striking originality.[25]

In the authentic text the expression '*ta panta*' = 'the universe'[26] appears only at the beginning of 5[18]. Yet why should the writer in a passage dealing especially with reconciliation mention in passing that the universe comes from God ('*ek tou theou*')?[27] It is as though he wanted to bar the way to a kind of Gnosticism which attributed creation to a demiurge working on his own account. It is God the Father also who takes the initiative in reconciliation.[28] Christ is distinguished from Prometheus, the crucified Greek, precisely by His entire accord with heaven. Remember the essential nature of the Apostle's doctrine of reconciliation.[29] Never is it said that God must be reconciled with man, even though the concept of divine wrath is

---

[24] There must have existed a reading '*kenē ktisis*,' to which '*ouk*' may have been added, for the 8th-century writer BEATUS HISPANUS has '*Non vacua creatura*,' cf. *Biblia Sacra*, 1915, p. 540. This edition of the Vulgate was not accessible to us, and since the edition of BEATUS in *MLS* 96, col. 985 reveals nothing of this we can only put on Windisch (p. 189) the responsibility for this piece of information. The original form of this variant therefore opposed the new creation to the old, which latter was of no more importance. But very probably it was simply an error of dictation, the diphthong '*ai*' being pronounced much like '*e*' (cf. Caesar = '*kaisar*'). Then '*ouk*' had to be added in order to assert something like the revaluation of the creature.

[25] The closest parallel to 5[17] is in the Apocalypse, Revelation 21[4-5], '*Ta prōta apēlthan . . . idou kaina poiō panta*' ('the first things are passed away . . . Behold, I make all things new'). But this lacks definite application to the individual existence of a Christian.—As for the reading in our verse '*gegonen kaina ta panta*' given by the Textus Receptus, it is perhaps due to later influence from Revelation.

[26] '*Ta panta*' is a technical expression for the universe, 'the All.' See our comments on this in the Commentary on 1 Corinthians *ad* 15[27].

[27] Remember the important distinction in 1 Corinthians 8[6] between '*ex hou*' and '*di' hou*.' God is the author of creation ('*ex hou*'), but it takes place through the mediation of the Son ('*di' hou*'), as in the Johannine Prologue. Similarly, reconciliation is brought about through the Son ('*dia Christou*', v. 18).

[28] What exactly is the force of '*hōs hoti*' at the beginning of v. 19, the obscurity of which has given much trouble to expositors (Bachmann: 'the obscure *hōs hoti*')? Loisy reads 'because'; NEB, 'what I mean is, that.' With Allo, we assume that once again (cf. 2[17]) '*hōs*' indicates a reason acknowledged by the subject. The minister is aware of being charged to announce that ('*hoti*').

[29] For the totality of his doctrine of reconciliation reference should be made to the commentaries on Romans, Galatians, and Colossians.—In the Epistle to the Ephesians, reconciliation is not between man and God, but between the two sections of humanity—Jew and Gentile.

(19) *For because God has reconciled the world to Himself in Christ—making no reckoning of their transgressions—He has also committed to us the proclamation of reconciliation.* (20) *We are therefore ambassadors in Christ's service, having the certainty that it is God who is addressing words of exhortation [to you] through us. We beg you therefore in Christ's name: Be reconciled to God.* (21) *He who did not know sin, God has identified with sin, so that we might become the justification of God in Him.*

not absent from the Pauline Epistles. But man, having fallen under the dominion of the devil and been enrolled, in some sense, in his army, has become God's enemy. He must therefore be torn away from this subjection, and it is this which is the essential feature of Paul's doctrine of the cross (particularly convincing texts are Colossians 1[13], 2[14-15]). Without this deliverance there would be neither the cancellation of sin's debt (*'mē logizomenos'*) nor justification. But in our passage the stress is upon the idea of the apostolic ambassador (*'presbeuomen'*) as the agent of the reconciliation (*'diakonia tēs katallagēs'*) which he proclaims (*'logos tēs katallagēs'*). It is interesting to observe the infrequency of diatribes full of threats directed against the sins of men, though such diatribes abound in the books of the prophets.

The expression *'en katallassōn,'* 5[19], literally 'was reconciling,' could be an Aramasism (as, for example, *'ēn esthiōn'* = 'he was eating,' in Mark 1[6]); *'kosmos'* in Paul's usage seems clearly to denote the 'universe' (including the angelic world).[30] But interest in our passage is focussed upon man.

5[20b] confirms our interpretation of reconciliation. It is man who must be reconciled to God (*'deometha, katallagēte'*), now that this has been made possible by justification (*'dikaiosunē'*, v. 21b). It is granted to us by God (*'theou'*) 'in Him'; it is even concisely expressed, no doubt by metonymy, in the words 'that we have become justification in him,' i.e. by our union with Christ, He having been 'made sin' for us. There is clearly no personification of sin here, still less of justification.[31] Nevertheless, the forcefulness of this paradoxical expression must not be ignored: Christ, though without sin (He did not know sin, *'ton mē gnonta hamartian'*) has been identified with sin. The *'ginōskō'* used here, like the Hebrew *'yaḍa''* ('to know'), denotes a practical or experiential knowing.[32]

Was this identification with sin achieved by the very incarnation in

[30] BACHMANN, p. 267, speaks of 'a world-embracing act of God.' On the other hand, GOGUEL expresses a measure of distrust with respect to the importance given to cosmology in systematising Pauline thought. See particularly *RPHR*, 1935, pp. 335–59. But he has not convinced us.

[31] The expression 'become justification' is doubtless more difficult than 'become sin.' It has been chosen to throw into relief the contrast between the two.

[32] Windisch refers to the use of *'ginōskō'* in Romans 7[7] and Revelation 2[24].

a 'body of death'?[33] The famous verse in Galatians 3[13], which quotes
Deuteronomy 21[23] ('cursed is every one that hangeth on a tree'),
makes us think that it is only in death that this mysterious identification—which in any case is far more than a simple imputation—is
accomplished. The Apostle appears to teach that it was necessary in
order to rescue humanity from domination by the devil.[34]

The least that one can say is that according to Paul Christ truly
burdened Himself with the sins of mankind. A. Schlatter has rightly
protested against the assimilation of Christ to Azazel[35] (Lev 16), yet
it is nevertheless very likely that Paul saw in this driving-away of sin
something akin to a prefiguration of its effacement by the mystery of
Golgotha (Col 2[14]). What is naturally true in Schlatter's observations is that the sacrifice of Christ far surpassed all the rites of the
Old Testament, because it involved the manifestation of the love of
God.

[33] John 1[29], in its customary interpretation ('who bears the sins of the world'),
seems to suggest an idea of this kind. But '*airōn tēn hamartian tou kosmou*' would
seem to mean rather 'He who brings to an end the sins of the world.' See C. H.
DODD, *The Interpretation of the Fourth Gospel*, Cambridge 1953, p. 237.

[34] Notice again that St Augustine has the following reading: 'Because he was
no sinner, on our behalf he made a sin offering.' This rests on a complete misunderstanding. Concerning '*hamartian epoiēsen*' Bengel pertinently remarks: 'Who
would have dared to speak in this way, unless Paul had said it first.'—Plummer,
p. 188, declares that 'St Paul's words here cannot be true, and yet it is possible
that they are the best way of stating what is true.'

[35] 'Ist Jesus ein Sündenbock?' *Kämpfende Kirche*, fasc. 22, undated.

CHAPTER VI

(1) *As co-workers [with Christ] we exhort you also not to receive the grace of God in vain. (2) For He says: 'In a time of acceptance I have answered you, and in a day of salvation I have helped you.' Behold, now is the time of welcome; behold, now is the day of salvation!*—(3) *We give no opportunity for scandal in any connection, in case our ministry should be derided;* (4) *but on the contrary, at every opportunity we give proof of ourselves as ministers of God: by great constancy in tribulations, hardships, agonies;* (5) *under blows, in imprisonments, in the*

6¹ '*Sunergountes*' = 'collaborating'. With whom? Chrysostom takes it as '*humin*' = 'with you', i.e. with the Corinthians.[1] But 5²⁰, where Paul represents himself as God's ambassador, suggests rather that '*tō theō*' (= 'with God') be understood—'fellow-worker *with God.*' It is this ministry which gives him authority to make the exhortations which follow.

Is '*dexasthai*' to be given a perfect meaning (= 'to have received') or a present (= 'to receive')?[2] The former creates difficulties, for how can anyone be exhorted not to have done something? It would be preferable to translate, as does the Synodale Version, 'act in such a way that you have not received the grace of God in vain ("*eis kenon*").' But, with the majority of commentators, we prefer the other translation, for acceptance of the Gospel is an action or state which continues.[3] This seems the more natural interpretation.

The Gospel would be accepted in vain if it produced no fruits.

6² We expect some more detailed exhortation, but the writer breaks off because the verb '*dexasthai*' = 'to receive' reminds him of an important biblical text which would serve to characterise the gravity of the existing situation. It comes from Isaiah 49⁸ and emphasises the arrival of the day of salvation. Reading between the lines it can be taken as an exhortation not to neglect this divine favour. The end of v. 2 expressly applies the text to the present time: 'behold, now ("*idou nun*" repeated twice) is the time!' But while the prophet speaks only of the time which has come ('*kairō dektō*' = lit. 'the moment to be accepted') the Apostle in his quotation gives this a little more stress by writing 'welcome' ('*euprosdektos*'), a nuance which translation must not lose.

---

[1] The Vulgate, by translating it as '*adjuvantes*', may suggest the same interpretation.

[2] Of course the aorist infinitive (and aorist participle also) does not necessarily imply action prior to that expressed by the main verb.

[3] Vulgate: '*ne recipiatis*,' etc.

midst of riots, in fatigue, in watchings, in fastings; (6) by purity, by knowledge, by patience, by kindliness, impelled by the Holy Spirit and by sincere love, preaching the word of truth, and sustained by the power of God. (7) We use the armour of righteousness, for attack and defence, (8) through honour or shame, through good or ill reputation; (9) taken for imposters, though true men; for unknown, yet well-known; as dying, and behold we live; as undergoing punishment, and yet not put to death;

6³, according to an old interpretation, which Luther revives, could be an exhortation to the Corinthians. That, indeed, might be expected here. But the Apostle is returning to the nature of his mission and the way in which he means to fulfil it. He avoids scandalising people so as not to expose himself to criticism. '*En mēdeni*' is often taken as masculine (Vulgate, Chrysostom, B.d.Cent.) = 'to no one.' But the proposition '*en*', and the parallel with '*en panti*' = 'in every way,' v. 4, makes us prefer the neuter 'in anything' (with Allo, Bachmann, Windisch, Plummer, Synodale Version).—'*Mōmeomai*' is reminiscent of *amōmos* = 'unblemished', and can mean 'to blame'—with a suggestion of the mockery which was not repugnant to the Greek spirit.

6⁴ᵇ (from '*en hupomonē*') to **6¹⁰** is classical, not only for its vigour and brilliance of style which ranks it with the finest rhetoric, but also for the strength of faith it expresses and the firmness of character revealed. The impression is given that in these burning paradoxes the depths of the Apostle's soul are being uncovered.

6⁴ᵇ, ⁵ '*Hupomonē*' = 'endurance' lacks co-ordination with the nouns which follow. The term denotes the attitude shown throughout the misfortunes enumerated in v. 4b,[4] which are grouped in threes. '*Anangkē*' = 'distress', 'anguish', and '*stenochōria*' = 'a situation of anguish' (cf. **4⁸** '*stenochōroumenoi*') are almost synonymous, the latter perhaps being the slightly stronger term. '*Plēgai*' = 'blows', see below, **11²⁵**. '*Akatastasiai*' = 'disorders'; '*agrupniai*' are involuntary deprivations of sleep; likewise '*nēsteiai*' = 'fastings' (from shortage of food).[5]

6⁶ The list in this verse is not a continuation of the catalogue of misfortunes (from '*thlipsesin*' to '*nēsteiais*'), but of the '*hupomonē*' of v. 5a; here we are informed of the reaction of the Apostle enabling him to triumph in these trials. The terms used present no difficulties, except perhaps for '*en logō alētheias*' = 'preaching the truth,' which must denote the imperturbable courage with which the Apostle continues his mission of preaching the Gospel.

[4] This catalogue of misfortunes is like a brief résumé of what is said (or rather: has been said) in **11²³ᶠ**.
[5] It is true that J. MÜLLER-BARDORFF, *TLZ* 1956, col. 347, appealing to Ephesians 6¹⁸ and Hebrews 13¹⁷, sees here the voluntary watchings and fastings which precede prayer. But the context does not favour this interpretation.

(10) *as plunged in grief, yet we are ever joyous; as beggars, but overflowing with wealth; as poverty stricken, yet possessing all things.* (11)
*We have spoken frankly to you, dear Corinthians. Our heart is wide
open [to you].* (12) *There is no constraint on our side; it is you who have
contracted your hearts.* (13) *I speak to you as to children. Respond as*

6⁷ (from '*dia*'; the break between v. 6 and v. 7 is ill made), first
mentions 'armour of the right and of the left'⁶ which the Apostle
uses, i.e. offensive arms (particularly the sword) and defensive (the
shield). Cf. **10⁴**, Eph 6¹⁶⁻¹⁷.

6⁸ takes up again the listing of vicissitudes. There are three antitheses:
'glory' and 'shame', 'bad' and 'good reputation', 'error' and 'truth'.

6⁹, ¹⁰ characterise, by new and striking antitheses, the contrast
between the visible appearance and the essential reality of the life of
the Apostle, which gives to carnal men the impression that he is in
the wrong. He seems to be unknown, or even to be rejected ('*ag-
nooumenoi*') viz. by God, like the 'servant' in Isaiah (cf. particularly
Isaiah 53²⁻³), whilst in reality he is favoured with the truth and recognised by God ('*epiginōskomenoi*'). He conveys the impression (and
from the fleshly point of view, a correct one) of being at the point of
death, of undergoing well-merited punishment,⁷ of being plunged
into grief ('*lupoumenoi*') and into beggary and misery⁸ ('*ptōchoi,
mēden echontes*'), and yet he is alive⁹ and overflowing with joy and
wealth to the extent of being able to enrich others ('*ploutizontes*').¹⁰
'*Idou*' = 'unexpectedly, contrary to anticipation' (Bengel).—It is
to be observed that some of the antitheses of v. 9—death, life; punishment, preservation from death—are reminiscent of Psalm 118
(117)¹⁷⁻¹⁸.¹¹

---

⁶ A current Greek expression. Windisch renders: 'weapons of offence and
defence.' It is pointless to invoke here the different estimate of right (the good
side) and left (the contrary).
⁷ Cf. Acts 28⁴.
⁸ '*Ptōchos*' = 'beggar', as in Luke 16²⁰ and probably also in Matthew 5³ and
Luke 6²⁰.
⁹ Having regard to the context we would think that '*zōmen*' not only alludes to
deliverances from the danger of death (11²⁴ᶠ ; 1 Cor 15³²; cf. Acts 19²³ᶠ) but also
and more particularly to the affirmation of the possession of a new and superior
life given through Christ.
¹⁰ It would be misguided to find here any hint of the collection for Jerusalem.
Clearly, it is a spiritual enrichment which is in mind. Nevertheless, the miraculous
success of the collection in the poor Church of Corinth could be looked upon as a
sign of their wealth of spiritual endowment.
¹¹ '*Ouk apothanoumai, alla zēsomai . . . paideuōn epaideusen me ho kurios, kai
tō thanatō ou paredōken me*' (' I shall not die, but I shall live . . . the Lord has
chastened me sorely, but He has not given me over to death'). The Apostle must
have had this text in mind.

they do by opening your own hearts [to us].—(14) *Do not form incongruous attachments with unbelievers; for what association can there be between light and darkness?* (15) *What accord between Christ and*

6[11–13] It is this same Psalm which, in the LXX Version, has some echoes of the affirmation in v. 11 '*hē kardia hēmōn peplatuntai*' = 'our heart is open to you,'[12] i.e. you have a large place in my heart. By analogy, '*to stoma aneōgen*,' 'my mouth is open to you,' means 'I am speaking to you frankly, with an open heart, hiding nothing of my life from you.' If the relations between writer and recipients are marred by some unease, it is because the latter do not act in the same way. Their 'bowels' are still, as it were, closed ('*stenochōreisthe*'). Let the warmth of their affection open their own hearts ('*platunthēte*', aorist middle of the verb '*platunō*', of which '*peplatuntai*' is the perfect);[13] this would re-establish the proper reciprocity between parent and children ('*tekna*', v. 13). '*Antimisthian*' = 'a service rendered in exchange for some other service.'[14]

The short paragraph 6[11–13] affects the transition to a parenetic pericope extending from 6[14] to 7[1], and, at first glance, it interrupts the apology, which is continued again at 7[2]. Yet it is closely linked to what precedes, as we have just seen, as well as to what follows (see below). It could therefore hardly be a supplement added after completion.

6[14a] The first recommendation, whose tenor is somewhat reminiscent of Leviticus 19[19] [15] and of Deuteronomy 22[10],[16] forbids collaboration with unbelievers. Is it a matter of forbidding mixed marriages? Probably so; but the prohibition must have a wider application, although no details are given.

6[14b] relates this prohibition to more general moral and theological truths, namely, to the incompatibility between justice and anarchy

---

[12] The Psalmist (LXX Ps 118[32]) says '*eplatunas tēn kardian mou*' ('thou enlargest my heart'), the subject being God.
[13] It goes without saying that '*peplatuntai*' is the third person *singular* (liquid stem).
[14] As BLASS–DEBRUNNER rightly observe (§ 154), the end of the phrase '*tēn autēn antimisthian . . . platunthēte*' could be regarded as a condensed expression representing '*ton auton platusmon platunthēte . . . hōs antimisthian*.'
[15] Leviticus 19[19] '*ta ktēnē sou ou katocheuseis heterozugō*' ('you shall not let your cattle breed with a different kind'); Vulgate: '*jumentum tuum non facies coire cum alterius generis animantibus*.'—According to Midrash Rabba on Genesis (FREEDMANN, p. 763) the existence of mules is contrary to the expressed will of the Creator.
[16] Deuteronomy 22[10] '*ouk arotriaseis en moschō kai onō epi to auto*' = 'you shall not plough with an ox and an ass together.' Both verses are here interpreted allegorically, rather like Deuteronomy 25[4] in 1 Corinthians 9[9].

Beliar? Or what alliance of believer with unbeliever? (16a) *What syncretism between the temple of God and idols?* (16b) *For we ourselves are the temple of the living God, as God has declared in these words: 'I will live and walk amongst them.—I will be their God, and they shall be my people.'* (17) *This is why he adds: 'Come out from the*

('*dikaiosunē*' and '*anomia*'; one could almost translate it as 'religion and atheism'), light and darkness, Christ and Beliar, believers and unbelievers, the temple of God and idols. 'Beliar' or 'Belial' was originally a common noun denoting a 'worthless' person, but in the pseudepigraphic literature, and notably in The Testaments of the Twelve Patriarchs, it came to signify Satan.[17] According to W. Bousset[18] the word here may denote the anti-Christ, i.e. a kind of eschatological incarnation of Satan, a view 'attractive rather than probable,' as Plummer says (p. 207).

6^{15-16} '*Sumphōnēsis*' = 'harmony', i.e. syncretism of Christian and pagan cults. For 'temple of God' ('*naos theou*') see also 1 Corinthians 3^{16}, 6^{19}, where, as here, the identity of the temple of God with 'us' i.e. with the Church,[19] is asserted. '*Zōntos*' is added to '*theou*', = 'of the living God,' as a reminder that God is the source of the new life.

6^{16b} is a reminiscence of Ezekiel 37^{27} combined with Leviticus 26^{12},[20] and it is connected particularly with the immediately preceding statement (Christians are the temple of God).

On the other hand, 6^{17} recalls biblical passages which should uphold the prohibition of mixing with unbelievers (cf. vv. 14, 15, and beginning of 16); the quotations are drawn from Isaiah 52^{11}, for the first three lines, and from Ezekiel 20^{34} for the last line.[21]

[17] Test. of Levi 19, Test. of Zebulun 9, and *passim;* for Satan see von Allmen, *Vocabulary of the Bible* (ET London 1958), art. Devil.
[18] *Die Schriften des N.T.*, 3rd edn 1917, II, p. 198.
[19] The Johannine equation is different: the temple of God = the body of Christ (Jn 2^{14-22}). Now, according to the Apostle Paul, we are the body of Christ (1 Cor 12^{27}). The circle is complete.—In our verse, 6^{16a}, some important witnesses, including p 46 and the Syriac Versions, read '*humeis*' for '*hēmeis*'; an interesting variant, which makes little difference to the sense. No words need be wasted over the confusion between 'u' and 'e', frequent in an age of itacism.
[20] '*Kai emperipatēsō en humin kai esomai humōn theos, kai humeis esesthe mou laos*' ('And I will walk amongst you and be your God, and you shall be my people'), Leviticus 26^{12}.—'*Kai estai hē kataskēnōsis mou en autois, kai esomai autois theos, kai autoi mou esontai laos*' ('And my dwelling shall be among them, and I will be their God, and they shall be my people'), Ezekiel 37^{27}.
[21] '*Apostēte, apostēte, exelthate, exelthate ekeithen, akathartou mē hapsēsthe, exelthate ek mesou autēs, aphoristhēte*' ('depart, depart, go out, go out thence, touch no unclean thing, go out from the midst of her, separate yourselves'), Isaiah 52^{11}.—'*Kai eisdexomai humas ek tōn chōrōn*' ('and I will gather you out of the countries'), Ezekiel 20^{34}. Here the verb '*eisdechomai*' (lit. = 'to welcome towards') must mean 'to take out,' viz. across the frontiers, i.e. out of the lands of the Dispersion.

midst of them and be separate. Touch no impure thing, and I will receive you.' (18) *'So I will be a father to you, and you will be to me sons and daughters,' says the almighty Lord.*

6[18] recalls Hosea 2[1] and 2 Kings (Heb Samuel) 7[14],[22] and to some extent also Isaiah 43[6].

The last three words of 6[18] occur so frequently in the Old Testament that it is irrelevant to cite a definite text for them, as Nestlé does. Notice merely that the mention of daughters of God (*'thugateras'*) has been added to the text by the Apostle to stress the equality of the sexes in the eyes of God (cf. 1 Cor 7).—That the recommendation to 'come out from their midst' must not be taken literally is clear from 1 Corinthians 5[10]: for good or ill, Christians are obliged to live in the world.

[22] Isaiah 43[6]: *'age tous hious mou apo gēs porrōthen kai tas thugateras mou ap' akrōn tēs gēs'* ('bring my sons from a far land and my daughters from the ends of the earth').—Hos 2[1] (cf. Heb Bible 1[10]): *'ekei klēthēsontai huioi theou zōntos'* ('there they shall be called sons of the living God').—2 Kings (Heb Bible 2 Sam) 7[14]: *'egō esoma ιautō eis patera kai autos estai moi eis huion'* ('I will be to him a father and he shall be to me a son').

CHAPTER VII

(1) *My good friends, as we are therefore the recipients of such promises, let us purify ourselves from all defilement of the flesh and of the spirit, and attain our sanctification in the fear of God.* (2) *Understand us properly. We have wronged no one, ruined no one, exploited no one.*

The two first verses of this chapter should be attached to what precedes.[1] It is a sequel to the exhortations of 6^{14-18}. For the expression 'possessing the promises' (*'echein epanggelias'*), cf. 1 Timothy 4^8 and Hebrews 7^6. *'Molusmos'* is a quite general word for any kind of 'defilement'; not only is *'sarkos'* added but also *'pneumatos'*, as a reminder that sins may be committed not by the 'body' only but also by the 'spirit'. In this place, therefore, *'sarx'* and *'pneuma'* do not denote two opposed principles of life, bad and good respectively, as customary in Pauline usage, but two spheres of man's life, the biological and the intellectual.[2]

'Epitelountes hagiōsunēn' = 'bringing holiness to perfection,' *'hagiōsunē'* here having an ethical sense (cf. 1 Pet 1^{16}). It cannot be denied that Paul's ethics is paradoxical, for on the one hand he attributes all good accomplished by Christians to the Holy Spirit, and on the other he exhorts Christians to sustained efforts in order to progress.[3] The theoretical solution of the antinomy is indicated by the ability attributed to believers of thwarting the Holy Spirit, apart from whom no good can be done; and the practical solution is supplied by a maxim which is not given by Paul yet which seems to be in line with his position, namely, act as if everything depended on us, but trust in God as if everything depended on Him.

7^2 *'Chōrēsate hēmas'* is usually translated as 'give us a place in your hearts.' This would then refer back to 6^{11} (*'peplatuntai,'* cf. *supra ad* 6^{11}). But if so, should not the Apostle have expressed himself more

---

[1] The subdivision into chapters dates from the thirteenth century. By and large, it was not ill done.

[2] If Marcion replaced *'pneumatos'* by *'haimatos'* it was not merely to reproduce the current locution *'sarx kai haima'* (cf. 1 Cor 15^{50}), but also because his dualism only allowed for sins of the body.

[3] Cf. WINDISCH, 'Das Problem des paulinischen Imperativs', *ZNTW*, 1924, pp. 265–81.—BULTMANN, 'Das Problem der Ethik bei Paulus,' *ibid.*, pp. 123–40.—L. H. MARSHALL, *The Challenge of N.T. Ethics*, London 1946, Ch. 7 onwards.—For *'en phobō'* (end of v. 1) p 46 has the curious reading *'en agapē.'* A Marcionite emendation? In any case, 'fear of the Lord' is quite in place here, cf. 5^{11}; Ephesians 5^{21}; Philippians 2^{12}.

(3) I am not saying this to condemn you. I have already declared that we bear you in our hearts in living and in dying. (4) I have great confidence in you. I am very proud about you. My heart is full of consolation and overflows with joy in the midst of all my afflictions. (5) In fact, when we arrived in Macedonia our poor body found no relief. Trials beset us —strife without, fears within. (6) But God, who comforts the humble,

clearly? We agree with Allo that it is more natural to let '*chōrein*' have the meaning it has customarily in the Gospels,[4] namely, 'to understand'; the Apostle exhorts his recipients to understand his intentions.—The three verbs '*adikeō*' = 'to wrong,' '*phtheirō*' = 'to ruin,' '*pleonekteō*' = 'to despoil' are almost synonymous. Had the writer wished to mark a gradation he would have put the second word at the end. He is reminding the Corinthians that he has scrupulously respected their proper rights (cf. below; 12^{11-18}).

7^3 Why does the writer stress that he does not want to be condemnatory ('*pros katakrisin ou legō*' = 'I do not speak by way of condemnation')? Since v. 2 might entail an allusion to persons (false apostles) who conducted themselves improperly, the author is anxious to make it clear that he is not reproaching the Church as a whole in any of this.—'To die and to live together' is not a specifically Christian way of speaking; pagans of every age have been able to unite together 'in life and death' ('for better, for worse').[5] Though here the bond of union, in particular between the Apostle and the Corinthians, being sealed by Christ, rises to a higher plane and excludes the loyalty through right and wrong ('*per fas et nefas*') so characteristic of paganism.[6]

7^4 '*Parrhēsia*' = 'confidence,' 'assurance,' as almost always.— '*Kauchēsis*' here = 'cause for boastfulness.'—The piled-up expressions, so characteristic of the Pauline touch,[7] will be noticed here: '*peplērōmai*' = 'I am filled with consolation' (active and passive sense) and '*huperperisseuomai*' = 'I abound and overflow with joy.'

---

[4] Matthew 19^{11-12}, '*chōrein*' = 'to understand' in an intellectual sense; Mark 2^2 ('to advance'); John 2^6, 21^{25} ('to hold'), in a physical sense.

[5] HORACE, Carmina 3, 9, 24: '*tecum vivere amem, tecum obeam libens,*' 'with thee I would live, and with thee gladly die' (cited by Wettstein).—Nicolas of Damascus (according to Athenaeus) characterised the *Ambacti* Gauls (cf. CAESAR, Gallic War, III, 22) as '*sunzōntas kai sunapothanountas,*' 'living together and dying together' (a reference borrowed from the learned and enjoyable article of F. OLIVIER, '*Sunapothnēskō*', RTP, 1929, pp. 103–33).

[6] E.g. the famous 'Nibelungen-Treue', which was no more than the collusion of an assassin and his accomplice (Hagen and Gunther).

[7] For '*perisseuō*' cf. TWNT VI, p. 38, and the literature referred to there.

comforted us by the arrival of Titus; (7) and not merely by his arrival, but by the encouragement he had received from you. For he reported to us your ardent desire [to see us again], your tears, your keen affection for me, so that my joy increased still more; (8) for even if I saddened you by my letter, I do not regret it; and even if I did regret it—for I see that the letter caused you sorrow, if only for a short time—(9) I rejoice now, not that you were made sorrowful, but that your sorrow drove you to repentance. For your sorrow was a religious sorrow and such that you suffered no harm from us. (10) For religious sorrow produces contrition, which leads to salvation and leaves no place for any

7⁵ The author here takes up again the narrative of his journey to Macedonia, broken off at 2¹⁴. **7⁵** recalls 2¹³, except that '*pneuma*' is replaced here by '*sarx*', 'my flesh found no relief,' '*sarx*' indicating the sum of all the circumstances of daily life (as in 1 Cor 7²⁸). The Apostle's existence was buffeted by struggles ('*machai*') with (unnamed) adversaries, as well as by 'fears' ('*phoboi*'), i.e. states of depression, perhaps caused by illness.

7⁶⁻⁷ However, the return of Titus as a bearer of good tidings brought him comfort. Well received by the Corinthians, he was able to express their ardent longing ('*epipothēsis*') to see the Apostle again, their tender solicitude ('*odurmos*', lit. = 'lamentation'), their keen affection ('*zēlos*'). The letter referred to in what follows (7⁸ᶠᶠ) seems, therefore, to have arrived at Corinth before Titus and to have taken effect.⁸

7⁸ The author does not regret, or no longer regrets, having caused sorrow ('*elupēsa*') to his recipients. If there have been regrets (v. 8b) they belong to the past, because they were effaced by joy. This is the general tenor of v. 8b, though it presents some difficulties. The construction is somewhat tortuous. The phrase from '*blepō*' to '*humas*' must doubtless be regarded as a parenthesis, the '*nun chairō*'⁹ = 'now (in the present) I rejoice' being a normal apodosis to '*ei kai metemelomēn*' = 'even if I regretted it.' The parenthesis explains why the Apostle may have had regrets: he realised—after the event—that his letter could wound his recipients, even if only for a short time ('*ei kai pros hōran*').¹⁰

⁸ There is, then, no real reason for doubting the identification of this letter with the 'sorrowful letter' mentioned in 2⁴ᶠᶠ.

⁹ This is why we do not accept G. Godet's attractive explanation. He attaches '*ei kai metemelomēn*' to what precedes.

¹⁰ Nestlé's text reads '*blepō*' (without '*gar*') after '*metemelomēn*'. But this rather unsatisfactory reading is supported only by B and D. The majority of other witnesses read '*blepō gar*.' But the best reading is perhaps that of p 46, which is implied also by the Vulgate: '*blepōn*' = 'seeing that.' It easily explains the other two. The final 'n' of the participle may have been lost, and the '*gar*' added later in consequence.

regret, whilst profane sorrow leads to death. (11a) *You see, then, what eagerness that religious sorrow produced for you, what excuses, what indignation, what fear, what longing, what ardour, what concern for justice!* (11b) *In every respect you have shown yourselves irreproachable in this affair.* (12) *Therefore, although I wrote to you* [*in that way*], *we were nevertheless comforted, not, of course, because of the wrongdoer, nor because of the wronged, but precisely because your solicitude*

7^{9-10} make a further discrimination of the highest importance. There are two kinds of sorrow, a 'godly sorrow' ('*hē kata theon lupē*') and a 'worldly sorrow' ('*hē tou kosmou lupē*'). We should not be wrong in thinking of the former as what later was called contrition. Indeed, Paul expressly says that it produces a repentance ('*metanoia*') which leads to salvation (v. 10a). The other kind of sorrow, which is profitless and leads to death, is certainly something like simple attrition or affliction.

Certain details need further clarification. At the end of v. 9b it is said that 'godly' sorrow, i.e. experienced in relation to God, has saved the Corinthians from loss ('*zēmiōthēnai*'). What was the nature of this harm? Perhaps Paul would not have returned to Corinth.

In 7^{10} the adjective '*ametamelēton*' = 'what is not regretted' can be attached either to '*metanoian*' = 'to repent,' or to '*sōtērian*' = 'salvation'. The latter would give a most banal assertion: one will not regret salvation. The former imparts an interesting intuition, namely, that genuine repentance creates a new situation which transforms the past, and leaves no room for regrets[11] (*sic* Windisch, Synodale Version).

7^{11} comments approvingly on the signs of amends among the Corinthians, following their true '*metanoia*', and implying a genuine turning again to himself: eagerness ('*spoudē*' and '*zēlos*') for the right, excuses ('*apologia*'), indignation ('*aganaktēsis*') with the sinner who had disturbed the Church, their decision to apply punishment ('*ekdikēsis*'), their desire to see the Apostle once more ('*epipothēsis*').[12] The word '*phobos*' = 'fear' needs explanation. Was it fear of the Apostle, as v. 15 might suggest? But it could be, as it seems to us more likely, the fear of God, which brought them again into the right road.—The end of v. 11 reaches a conclusion which is, in a way, a verdict of

---

[11] The rhythm of the sentence, when read aloud, likewise impels us to attach '*ametameleton*' to '*metanoian*'. But we realise how very subjective this argument is.—Windisch thinks that the Apostle's thought would have been clearer if he had chosen '*ametanoēton*' = 'requiring no second repentance.' But this idea does not seem to be suggested by the context.

On the transformation of the past by repentance cf. MAX SCHELER, 'Renaissance et Repentir' in the collection *Le sens de la souffrance*, Paris 1936.

[12] '*Alla*' here means 'not only this, but also.' See BLASS–DEBRUNNER, § 448. 6

for us was clearly shown among you before God. (13) *But in addition to this comfort we have had a greater and more abundant cause for joy in the joy Titus experienced from the consolation his spirit received from you all.* (14) *For I was somewhat boastful about you to him, and I have not been put to shame. For as on every occasion we have told you the truth, the boasting which we made to Titus has been shown equally well-founded.* (15) *And his affection for you has redoubled; for he remembers the obedience of you all and how you received him with fear and trembling.* (16) *I rejoice that I can rely upon you on every occasion.*

acquittal. As a whole, the Church was not defiled by or in this affair ('*tō pragmati*,' or '*en tō pragmati*' according to the Textus Receptus), '*pragma*' being, in reality, a legal term.

7^{12} is somewhat reminiscent of 2^9. But is it correct, as is usually done, to link all the rest of v. 12 to 'although (or: even if?) I wrote to you' ('*ara ei kai egrapsa humin*')? Was the Apostle really able to say that he did not write the letter because of the wrongdoer and his victim? This interpretation seems very awkward and hence we prefer, with Ch. Bruston,[13] to attach this passage—from '*ouch heneken*' to '*enōpion tou theou*'—to what follows, viz. to '*parakeklēmetha*' = 'we were comforted,' by putting a comma before this verb.[14] The meaning would then become wholly acceptable. The Apostle says that, although he had written the letter in sorrow, he had been comforted, not by the attitude of the wrongdoer or the wronged party, but by the zeal of the Corinthians for himself ('*phanerōthēnai tēn spoudēn humōn pros hēmas*') before God ('*enōpion theou*'). As Ch. Bruston remarks, this translation allows us to keep for the whole passage the usual sense of '*heneken*', which in the New Testament almost always has purely causal and not final force, which latter it would have in the customary translation according to which the Apostle says 'I wrote that letter with a view to, or in order to provoke the zeal of the Corinthians.'[15]

'*Pros humas*' near the end of 7^{12} can only mean 'with you.'[16] But we would prefer to read '*en humin.*'

---

[13] *Les trois Epîtres de l'apôtre Paul conservées par l'Eglise*, Paris 1917, p. 10.
[14] The break between v. 12 and v. 13 should have been made after '*parakeklē-metha.*'
[15] Among the texts cited by Bruston in this connection we have reservations about Romans 8^{36} '*heneken sou thanatoumetha*,' a quotation from Psalm 44^{23}, as well as Romans 14^{20}: do not destroy the work of God because of a matter of food ('*heneken brōmatos*'). We could add numerous texts from the Synoptic Gospels where '*heneken*' lacks any final force—persecuted for righteousness' sake, for the sake of the Son of Man, &c. (always '*heneken*'), as well as Acts 26^{21}, 28^{20}.
[16] '*Pros*' with the accusative in the sense of 'with', 'by', is, of course, encountered in John 1^1.

7¹³ Not Paul alone, but Titus also experienced joy and comfort from the attitude of the Corinthians (*'chara'*, *'anapepautai'*), as they fell in again behind his (Titus') master.

7¹⁴ recalls that Paul had commended this companion, as he had commended Timothy in 1 Corinthians 16¹⁰. He had no reason to be ashamed (*'ou katēschunthēn'*) of his praise. He had spoken truly of things, as on all other occasions (*'panta'*).

7¹⁵ Titus felt genuine affection for them; *'splangchna'* = 'bowels', i.e. the seat of loving feelings.[17] What is strange is that the Corinthians received him 'with fear and trembling' (*'meta phobou kai tromou'*), and that Titus was particularly glad about it. Should *'hōs'* = 'as' be taken as weakening the following phrase (= 'almost')? But this use of *'hōs'* is rare, so that it is best to let it have causal force here (= 'because').[18]

7¹⁶ again stresses the Apostle's joy, provoked by the confidence (*'tharrō'*) which he can have in them. The confidence is similarly well-founded, for Paul, even less than the other Apostles, taught no blind confidence in people, even if they were Christians.[19]

---

[17] Often *'splangchna'* = 'compassion'. There is no need to say that Hebrew psycho-physiology differed widely from our own. Cf. R. EPPEL, 'Le piétisme juif dans les Testaments des douze patriarches,' *EHPR*, 22, 1930, pp. 111–23. One laughed with the spleen, thought with the kidneys and heart, &c.

[18] Windisch observes that *'meta phobou kai tromou'* often describes the attitude of the religious man before the *numinosum*. The idea would perhaps have surprised Titus, that he was identified with a *numen*.

[19] We have already observed elsewhere (in connection with an erroneous translation of 1 Corinthians 13⁵) that the morality (and diplomacy!) of unconditional trust is anti-biblical, particularly in relation to wolves and false-prophets. See our Commentary on 1 Corinthians, and our publication *A good and a bad Government according to the New Testament* (American Lecture Series 221, Springfield, Illinois, 1954).

CHAPTER VIII

(1) Dear brothers, we wish to make you acquainted with the grace which God has bestowed on the Churches of Macedonia. (2) Tested by a serious adversity, they made their extreme poverty issue into treasures of generosity with overflowing joy. (3) For—I am their witness in this— [they gave] according to their means, and even beyond their means and cheerfully, (4) asking us insistently for the privilege of taking part in the collection for the Christians [at Jerusalem]. (5) They even surpassed our hopes, but they first offered themselves to God and then to us by the will of God. (6) And so we have requested Titus to guide this work of

Chapters **8** and **9** deal with practical questions only, namely the matter of the collection for the 'saints' (*'hagioi'*), that is, the Christians in Jerusalem.

The Apostle begins with praise for the generosity of the Churches in Macedonia, doubtless those at Thessalonica, Philippi and Beroea, and of others, perhaps, of which we know nothing. He then examines the question from several viewpoints and takes advantage of the opportunity to commend the messengers whom the Corinthians do not yet know.

8[1] *'Charis'* here = a special 'grace' given by God (*'dedomenēn'*), or more exactly spread among the Churches (*'en tais ekklēsiais'*).[1]

8[2-4] tells us that the Macedonians have suffered difficulties, during which they have been tested (*'dokimē thlipseōs'*). We are also told that they were 'abjectly poor' (*'hē kata bathous ptōcheia'*).[2] Nevertheless, they had shown themselves very generous (*'eperisseusen'*). The expression *'eis to ploutos tēs haplotētos'* = lit. 'for the wealth of the charity' is rather condensed; it must refer to the result of their generosity, namely the size of the collection.[3] The Macedonians have given not merely 'according to their means' (*'kata dunamin'*), but beyond them (*'para dunamin'*). They have not contributed then from their surplus but from their necessity, like the widow in Mark

---

[1] *'En'*, according to BLASS–DEBRUNNER § 220. 1, may have here the sense of 'for', 'on behalf of'; this would cause no problem.

[2] We may wonder whether Macedonia had been especially tested by the earthquakes which, in the time of Claudius, shook certain provinces. But we have not found any information on this point in Pliny the Elder or in Tacitus.

[3] *'Haplotēs'* can mean piety in general; here it refers to liberality to the brethren as in 9[11,13] and Romans 12[8].—In the Testaments of the Twelve Patriarchs this virtue plays a very important part. See especially Test. of Issachar, Chapter 4, where it implies purity of heart primarily. Other texts are mentioned by R. EPPEL, 'Le piétisme juif dans les Testaments des douze Patriarches,' *EHPR*, 22, 1930, Ch.3.

*charity among you to a happy conclusion with the same success as he
began it.* (7) *Now, as you excel in all things, in faith, eloquence, knowledge, boundless zeal and in the love which we have communicated
to your hearts, be just as generous in this work of charity.* (8) *I am not
saying this as an order, but, by setting before you the example of others,
as a means of providing the opportunity for you to show the sincerity of
your charity also.* (9) *For you know the unselfishness of our Lord Jesus
Christ; He who was rich, made Himself poor for you, in order to enrich
you by His poverty.* (10) *It is then merely a word of advice which I am*

12⁴¹⁻⁴.—'*Authairetoi*' should not be translated as 'spontaneously';
for vv. 3 and 4 remind us that the collection had been made at Paul's
request. This adjective should remind us that they acted in 'good heart,'
without pressure.

8⁵ repeats that the result surpassed all hopes. This heart-warming
fact arises because the Christians first of all 'gave themselves to the
Lord' ('*heautous edōkan prōton tō kuriō*'), that is by approaching God
through prayer, and He replied by urging them to give themselves to
us ('*kai hēmin dia thelēmatos theou*').

8⁶ The handsome success encouraged the Apostle to send Titus to
Corinth to bring the task of the collection ('*charis*') which he had
begun earlier to its conclusion, a remark which refers to this evangelist's earlier journey, mentioned in 7,⁴ and without doubt also in
the separate note, written earlier, which is now 9 (see Introduction).

8⁷ The Apostle expresses the conviction that their charity ('*charis*')
will be on a par with their faith ('*pistis*'), their eloquence ('*logos*'),
their theological knowledge ('*gnōsis*'), their religious zeal ('*spoudē*')
and their Christian love; this last is denoted by the rather curious
turn of phrase ('*tē ex hēmōn en humin agapē*,' which probably signifies: the love which is in you and which I inspired in you.⁵

---

⁴ The advice given in 1 Corinthians 16² not to wait for the last moment, but to
give each Sunday a certain sum, set aside during the week, can be explained by
the Church's relative poverty.
⁵ Many witnesses, and not unimportant ones (S, C, D, among others) read, '*ex
humōn en hēmin*' = 'our love inspired by you,' the reading adopted by Tischendorf. But here it is not Paul's attitude which is in question. The Vulgate reads:
'*caritate vestra in nos.*' This variant would give excellent sense—'your charity
towards us'—but would presuppose '*agapē humōn eis hēmas*' (or '*pros hēmas*'), a
reading unsupported by any Greek manuscript. Again itacism!—On what does
the '*hina*' at the end of v. 7 depend? The verb '*parakalesai*' is at a considerable
distance (beginning of v. 6). It must be postulated that a repetition of this verb
('*parakalō*') is understood, or that '*hina*' with the subjunctive is merely a way of
expressing the imperative, as in French ('qu'il s'en aille'). See BLASS–DEBRUNNER,
§ 387.3. Modern Greek does the same thing: '*na*' with subjunctive = imperative.

*giving you; for it will be in keeping with your conduct, you who were the
first to undertake this work, and even to decide on it, as long ago as last
year.* (11) *Now finish the work, so that the performance matches the
eagerness of your resolution, according to your means.* (12) *For if good*

8[8] The Apostle does not wish to give an order (*'ou kat' epitagēn legō'*),
but a piece of advice (see **8**[10], *'gnōmēn didōmi'*). However, he cannot
prevent himself from stating that the collection will be a proof
of the Corinthians' charity; *'dokimazō'* = 'to put to the test'; *'to
agapēs gnēsion'* = 'the genuineness of the charity,' rather as the
Sorrowful Letter had been a proof of their eagerness to do good (**7**[12]).

8[9] gives a brief Christological digression, which is rather like a partial
recapitulation of the well-known passage in Philippians 2^{5-11}. As in
that passage, the attitude of Christ is given as an example and special
stress is laid on His poverty (*'eptōcheusen'*). Together with the majority of exegetes,[6] we are of the opinion that the riches (*'ploutos'*)
which Christ gave up refer to His pre-existent status. However,
'eptōcheusen' = lit. 'made himself a beggar' evokes not only the
inferiority of the human condition as such, but also (without the
Apostle thinking particularly about it) the life of 'the poor' (the
"ebyonîm"), for whom Jesus had much sympathy and whose existence
He largely shared. The choice of phrase is therefore a particularly
happy one.

8[10] contains two difficulties. Firstly, what is the meaning of *'touto
humin sumpherei'* = lit. 'this is useful to you'? Is it the Apostle's
advice or the collection itself that will be 'useful' to them, because
their moral and religious standard will be raised thereby? But in that
case, could the Apostle not have expressed himself more clearly? We
prefer to recall as does Liddell–Scott that *'sumpherei'* can quite
normally mean 'this is expedient,' that is to say that the Apostle
thinks it reasonable to limit himself to a simple piece of advice, in
view of their zeal.— Furthermore, why is the *decision* to take part in
the collection (*'to thelein'*) apparently considered as more important
than its execution (*'to poiēsai'*)? The fact that both carry us back to
the previous year (*'proenērxasthe apo perusi'*[7] = 'you started this

[6] Cf. our article 'Kyrios Anthropos,' *RHPR*, 1936, pp. 196ff.
[7] The adverb *'perusi'*, derived apparently from *'para'* and *'etos'* (?), means: in
the course of the past year; *'apo perusi'* means approximately the same thing. It is
therefore a term which lacks precision. *'Perusi'*, again preceded by *'apo'*, occurs
again in **9**[2], but is not found elsewhere in the Bible.

*will is not lacking, the result will be received with pleasure, account
being taken of what you have—and there is no question about what you
do not have.* (13) *Indeed, it is not a matter of reducing yourselves to
penury, in order to relieve others. The ideal is equality.* (14) *In the
present case, your abundance will offset their need, so that [one day]
their abundance may offset your need,* (15) *according to this scriptural
text: 'He who had collected much did not have too much, and he who
had collected but little lacked nothing.'* (16) *May thanks be given to God
therefore who puts into the heart of Titus the same solicitude for you.*

very thing moving a year ago') does not overcome the difficulty. It is
pointless to list the explanations of commentators, who are in
general quite perplexed. We think that perhaps the Apostle wishes to
praise the Corinthians for having the idea themselves, before being
exhorted to it.

8[11] Here the Apostle exhorts them to complete what they had so well
begun. But what is the meaning of '*ek tou echein*'? By taking 'out of
what they have'? That would be a very banal statement. Perhaps
Windisch is right in supposing that the Apostle, through discretion,
does not wish to ask his flock for as superhuman an effort as that of
the Macedonians.

Indeed, 8[12] underlines that goodwill ('*prothumia*') is the essential
thing, and that no one will be criticised if his modest means do not
allow exceptional sacrifices; he is not expected to give 'in proportion
of what he does not have' ('*ou katho ouk echei*').

8[13–15] It is not a question of spoiling the Greeks to enrich the Judaeans. Equality ('*ex isotetos*') should rather be the ideal. 8[15] quotes a
text from Exodus (16[18]), which speaks of a certain equality in the
gathering and distribution of the manna in the desert.
　What is more curious is that the end of 8[14] seems to hint that the
Jerusalem Christians might one day have the opportunity of doing
likewise for the Corinthians. Doubtless this is rather a theoretical
possibility or a pure demand of principle, in view of their chronic
poverty.

8[16–21] These verses speak further of the new mission of Titus and the
despatching of other delegates.

8[16–17] The author gives prominence to Titus' eagerness to return to
Corinth, prompted by the warm welcome he had found there. What
is less easily understood is the further delay of the Apostle's own
journey, since the reasons given in **2** have been set aside after his reconciliation with the Corinthians. It can only be supposed that the

(17) For he accepted my request, and showing lively eagerness, readily came to you, (18) and we have sent with him the brother whose high repute as an evangelist has spread through all the Churches. (19) And furthermore, he was selected by the vote of the Churches as our travelling companion in this charitable work which we are undertaking for the glory of the Lord and for our own satisfaction. (20) We are taking these precautions so that nothing can be said against us about the contributions of which we have charge. (21) For we seek what is good, not only in the sight of God but also of men. (22a) And with them we

work in the Macedonian Churches had detained him further. Perhaps he also wished to be as little as possible involved in the collection, in order to give no grounds for the ever-present possibility of calumny. This preoccupation will indeed be made explicit in **8²⁰**, in which he explains that he has taken the precaution of entrusting the collection to others so as not to be suspected (*'mē tis hēmas mōmēsētai'*), and the more so as the collection was to bring in large sums.

8¹⁸ᶠ speak of a 'brother' (*'adelphos'*), known for his missionary zeal who was apparently chosen by a show of hands (*'cheirotonētheis'*) by the 'Churches' (in Macedonia no doubt) to accompany Paul (*'sunekdēmos'*) and to help him in his work. The expression *'sunekdēmos hēmōn'* suggests that he must have set off with Paul, but may also refer to the journey from Corinth (where the Apostle was to join him) to Jerusalem. What is more curious is the anonymity of this brother. If *'adelphos'* should designate 'the *brother* of Titus,' why is his name not given? Suggestions have included Luke, Barnabas, and Aristarchus, called the Macedonian and *'sunekdēmos Paulou'* in Acts 19²⁹ (cf. Acts 27² where he is clearly stated to be a Thessalonian, also Acts 20⁴ ⁸). But none of these hypotheses explains the anonymity. Therefore the supposition must be seriously considered that the name was erased because the evangelist, whoever he was, forfeited his credit later on.⁹

8²⁰ *'Hadrotēs'* (from *'hadros'* = 'vigorous', 'full-grown') = 'abundance'.—Among the many meanings of the verb *'stellomai'*, there is

---

⁸ For Luke: ORIGEN, *Homily I on Luke* (Opera vol. 9, p. 10 in *GCS*), followed, among others, by JEROME, *De viris* 7 (*MPL*, 23, col. 620), and in modern times by Bachmann. The silence of Acts could, at a pinch, be explained by the ingenious hypothesis advanced by E. TROCMÉ ('Le Livre des Actes et l'Histoire,' *EHPR*, 45, 1957); according to this the friend of Theophilus (distinct from Luke) would have at his disposal only some fragmentary diaries of Luke's.—For Barnabas: CHRYSOSTOM *ad loc.* (*MPG*, 61, col. 524), followed by THEODORET (*MPG*, 82, col. 428).— For Aristarchus, TH. ZAHN, *Einleitung in das Neue Testament*, I, 1897, pp. 228f, and in a moderate way WINDISCH, p. 264.—For the brother of Titus: SOUTER, *ET* 18, pp. 280ff and 335ff. According to this writer Titus' brother was Luke. This would bring us back to the first hypothesis.

⁹ It is difficult to understand why Windisch, who shares this opinion, nevertheless appears to opt for Aristarchus. Then why should his name not have been erased also from the Acts?

*have sent our brother whose diligence we have often proved in many
ways,* (22b) *and who in the present case is even more keen because of the
profound confidence which he holds in you.* (23) *As for Titus, he is my
associate and my fellow-worker among you. As for our brothers, they
are the delegates of the Churches, they are doing honour to Christ.*
(24) *Give them the proof of your charity and of the good grounds for
our praise of you, in the eyes of the other Churches.*

one which is a pure invention of modern scholars—'to fear.' The
sense of 'avoid' (Vulgate: *'devitantes'*) could be justified if the verb, as
in 2 Thessalonians 3[6] or Malachi 2[5], were constructed with *'apo'*,
which is certainly not the case here. Here we prefer to give to *'stellomai'* the sense of 'to set out upon a task,' 'to undertake,' attested by
Estienne and Liddell–Scott, and to explicate as follows: Paul had
organised 'this thing,' that is the collection (with all the precautions),
so as not to have his honesty suspected in any way. Indeed, says the
continuation (8[21]), even the semblance of anything which is not good
must be avoided, as is expressed in the maxim in Proverbs 3[4] (LXX).[10]

8[22] mentions a third delegate, of whose zeal he boasts, a zeal increased (*'spoudaioteron'*) by confidence (*'pepoithēsei'*) in the Corinthians. Windisch here thinks primarily of Luke. But why is he not
mentioned by name? It has also been supposed that becase he is called
'adelphos hēmōn' = 'our brother' he might be a near-relative of the
Apostle's (brother or cousin);[11] but in that case, would there not be
the additional *'kata sarka'* = 'according to the flesh,' in its natural
sense? Perhaps his name has also been erased.

8[23] restates that all missionaries work for the glory of Christ (*'doxa
Christou'*). Moreover, *'apostoloi'* seems to have here the sense of
'delegates' (of the Churches) and not the strong sense of 'Apostles'.

8[24] contains a philological problem: where is the finite verb? An
'este' = 'be' must be understood after *'endeiknumenoi'* = 'proving',
or alternatively *'endeixesthe'* = 'prove'[12] must be read.

[10] *'Kai pronoou kala enōpion kuriou kai anthrōpōn'* ('and provide for things
honourable in the sight of the Lord and men'). Cf. CICERO, *De officiis* II, Ch.
21, § 75, 'But the chief thing in all public administration and public service is to
avoid even the slightest suspicion of self-seeking.'—The Christian should of
course know how to bear calumny; the whole Epistle teaches this. But he will not
provoke it gratuitously, especially if his work might suffer as a consequence.
[11] Bleek is claimed by WINDISCH to have advanced this hypothesis, p. 266.
Obviously it is not absolutely beyond possibility, in view of our ignorance of
Paul's family. We should not know that he had a sister and nephew (in Jerusalem) if they were not incidentally named in Acts 23[16–17]; but it would be curious
if no tradition or legend had seized on the figure of a brother of Paul, who was also
a missionary.
[12] With S, C, Vulgate, the Coptic Versions, the Peshitta and the Textus Receptus (according to Tischendorf). This variant is therefore not badly attested, but
could represent an emendation.

Also to be noted is the 'etymological figure' *'endeixin endei-knumenoi'* which is difficult to translate. In any event it is clear that the recommendation is addressed to the Corinthians, who will have to prove 'in the eyes of the Churches' (*'eis prosōpon tōn ekklēsiōn'*) their affection (*'agapē'*) and justify the praise (*'kauchēsis'*) which has been uttered on their account.

CHAPTER IX

(1) *It is unnecessary for me to write to you about the collection for the benefit of the Christians [in Jerusalem].* (2) *For I know your goodwill which I boast about to the Macedonians by saying that Greece has been ready since last year; and the fact is that your enthusiasm has been a stimulus for the majority.* (3) *However, I have sent the brethren to you, so that the boast which I have made about you may not be belied on this point, and that you may be ready as I declared.* (4) *Otherwise, if the Macedonians come with me and catch you unprepared, we—not to mention you [as well]—should be abashed in such an eventuality.* (5) *I*

This chapter gives fresh exhortation with regard to the collection. The exhortation is surprising, for discussion of this topic seemed closed by the final remark in 8²⁴.[1] What is more surprising is that the tone of 9¹ seems to introduce a fresh topic not yet dealt with. One cannot get rid of the impression that 9 does not form the natural sequel to 8.[2] However, there is nothing to indicate that this note could have been sent to another Church, as Semler suggests. If a hypothesis is permissible, we think that it was sent to Corinth at almost the same time as the letter comprising 1–8, which was written slightly later. It can then be understood that both letters, received almost simultaneously, were put together into the Church's archives.

9¹⁻² again refer to the praise of the Corinthians given in the Churches of Macedonia (cf. 8²⁴); 'apo perusi' = 'last year' as in 8¹⁰. 'Erethizō' = 'promote healthy rivalry,' among the members of the Church no doubt.[3]

9³⁻⁴ 'Kenoō' = 'to empty,' 'to make empty,' 'to belie.' The 'brothers' mentioned here are not, in our interpretation, identical to those in 8. Nor does 'epempsa' = 'I have sent to you' necessarily refer to an earlier delegation. It is merely the past tense of a letter-writer, who places himself in the situation (future) of the recipients.

---

[1] Many translators write here (9¹) 'it is not necessary to say *more* to you.' We may be permitted to remark that this interpolation only masks the difficulty.

[2] This is the opinion of Semler, Windisch, Bruston and many others also. Indeed, Bruston places 9 after 13¹⁰.

[3] Windisch thinks that the zeal of the Corinthians was calculated to spur on the Macedonians, but he has to admit that this interpretation contradicts the developments in 8¹⁻⁵, where the opposite is clearly stated.

*have therefore thought it necessary to invite our brothers to come to you
ahead of me, and to organise in advance that bounty [already] announced, so that it may be ready and may represent liberality and not
niggardliness. (6) Look: he who sows scantily will reap scantily, and he
who sows generously will also reap generously. (7) Let each one give*

The Corinthians will have to be ready, when Paul and the Macedonians arrive.[4] '*Kataischunō*' as always = 'to put to shame,' 'dis-
honour'. The Apostle ('*hēmeis*') would be mortified by a lack of
response in the collection, and the Corinthians ('*humeis*') would cover
themselves with shame.

But what is the meaning of '*en tē hupostasei tautē*' at the end of
v. 4? It is known that in the Epistle to the Hebrews (11[1]) this word
('*hupostasis*') has its philosophical connotation = 'substance,' a
sense which is inadmissible here. Windisch is undecided between 'in
this connection' and 'in this matter.' But neither of these senses is
justified philologically. We think that '*hupo-stasis*' must be taken in its
etymological sense = 'supposition'. The fear is justified only if one
supposes the eventuality of a failure, the hypothetical nature of which
the author wishes to underline.

9[5] '*Pro-elthein*' = 'to precede.' Therefore a first embassy is in fact in
question. '*Katartisai*' = 'to arrange,' 'put in hand.' '*Pro*' = 'in
advance.' '*Eulogia*' is a rather solemn term for 'offering'.[5]

In v.5b '*eulogia*' = 'offering' viewed as 'largesse' is moreover contrasted with '*pleonexia*' = 'avarice'.[6] There is no question of thinking
oneself cleared of responsibility by giving the least possible sum.

9[6] As commentators have generally remarked, the Apostle here
applies an agricultural maxim to the fisco-moral realm: do not stint
in sowing in order to obtain a good crop.[7] '*Ep' eulogiais*' (twice) =

[4] It seems therefore to be supposed that Paul will accompany Titus and certain
delegates from Macedonia. According to **8** this is not so. It confirms our opinion
about the earlier date of **9**. Paul must have changed his plans between times.
  [5] The usual sense of '*eulogia*' in the LXX is 'blessing'. But sometimes the noun
is used for a solemn gift. In the case of Naaman's offering to Elisha, the offering
('*eulogia*') even has a religious tinge (2 Kings 5[15]). 1 Corinthians 16[1] uses '*logeia*'
for the collection.
  [6] The expression 'to give as largesse and not as avarice' is condensed; it would
not have displeased Tacitus who frequently wrote such sentences as: '*Reges ex
nobilitate, duces ex virtute sumunt*,' 'they take their kings on the ground of birth,
their generals on the basis of courage' (Germany, 7). We could have made a
similar remark about **5**[21].
  [7] Proverbs 22[8] had already applied a similar aphorism to the moral life: '*Ho
speirōn phaula therisei kaka*' ('he who sows the worthless shall reap the wicked').
Later, 'Solomon' says: '*Andra hilaron kai dotēn eulogei ho theos*' ('God blesses a
happy and generous man'), cf. **9**[7]. As for the agricultural rule in question, it may
perhaps have its roots in an agricultural religion, which forbids any tricking of
the god of the earth. Even today it is possible to meet peasants who consider it a
sin to plant cut potatoes.

according to the prompting of his heart, and not unwillingly or by constraint; for it is 'the cheerful giver whom God loves.' (8) *Now God has the power to overwhelm you with all benefits, so that while having at all times and in all circumstances the wherewithal to live, you may also have something left over for all good works.* (9) *Indeed it is written: 'He has distributed and given to the poor, His righteousness endures for ever.'* (10) *He who provides seed for the sower, and bread for food, will provide and multiply your seed and will cause the fruits of your righteousness to increase.* (11) *Thus you will be enriched in every way for all kinds of liberality, which through our intermediary will cause thanksgiving to rise to God.* (12) *For the service represented by this collection, has the effect not only of meeting the needs of the Christians [at Jerusalem], but will carry up to God a rich harvest of thanksgiving.*

'in a blessed manner,' that is abundantly; *'pheidomai'* here = 'to economise,' 'to stint.'

9⁷ Each will give according to his own decision (*'kathōs proērētai'*), without any sum being imposed. For the quotation (*'hilaron'*, etc.) see the preceding note.

9⁸⁻⁹ recall that Providence will perform a miracle (*'ho theos dunatei'*): the Corinthians, being generous themselves, will be showered with all good things (*'pasa charis'*). They will lack nothing (*'autarkeia'* = the situation of one who is self-sufficient, 'self-sufficiency') and will still be able to 'abound in all good works.' A quotation from Psalm 112⁹ (LXX) corroborates this view of things, which doubtless embraces spiritual as well as material matters.

9¹⁰ evokes a prophecy of Isaiah who praises the Lord who gives seed and bread.[8] The allusion to Hosea 10¹² at the end of v. 10 should make it clear that the present case bears primarily on the fruits of righteousness.[9]

9¹¹ adds a new idea: the gifts will call forth thanksgiving (*'eucharistian'*) to God. For *'haplotēs'* see under **8²**.

The participle *'ploutizomenoi'* has been taken in the passive sense = 'being showered with riches.' However, the middle sense, which can be confused with the active sense, is not altogether excluded— 'enriching' (others).

---

[8] Cf. Isaiah 55¹⁰, where the subject happens to be 'rain': *'ho huetos dōsei sperma tō speironti kai arton eis brōsin'* ('the rain will give seed to the sower and bread for food').

[9] Hosea 10¹²: *'Speirate heautois eis dikaiosunēn . . . ekzētēsate ton kurion heōs tou elthein genēmata dikaiosunēs humin'* ('sow for yourselves righteousness . . . seek the Lord until the fruits of righteousness come to you').

(13) *For the success of this collection will urge them to glorify God concerning your religious submission to the gospel of Christ, and your generous gift on their behalf and on behalf of all.* (14) *And they will show their affection for you by their prayers, because of the super-abundant grace of God which is resting upon you.* (15) *Thanks be to God for His unspeakable gift!*

9^{12-13} develops an idea already touched on in 9^{11}: the collection will not only provide for the needs of the 'saints' (*'husterēmata tōn hagiōn'*), but will call forth great thanksgiving from them. For the Corinthians, by the 'test' of the collection (*'dokimē tēs diakonias'*), will have proved two things: the submission of their religion to the gospel (*'hupotagē tēs homologias humōn eis to euanggelion tou Christou'*), and their generosity (*'haplotēs'*) towards the Jewish members and towards all.[10]

9^{14} discreetly expresses the hope of a tightening (or creation?) of bonds of affection between the Judaeans and the Greeks, or if it is preferred, between Judaeo-Christians and Gentile-Christians. *'Epipotheō'* = 'to desire,' 'to have a liking for' (cf. *'epipothēsis'*, $7^{7,11}$).

9^{15} concludes with a short doxology; one has the impression that the note is ended. *'Anekdiēgētos'* = 'inexpressible', a synonym for 'inexhaustible'.[11]

[10] We know nothing of a collection for others than the Jerusalemites. Doubtless the author wishes to stress that generosity could be practised in other similarly urgent cases. There is nothing partisan about it.—For *'homologia'* = 'religion', see also Hebrews 3^1; 4^{14}; 10^{23}.

[11] This is a biblical *hapax legomenon*, and rare elsewhere. It is found in the writings of Clement of Rome (1 Cor 49^4 and 61^1), but this does not mean that he knew our Epistle.

CHAPTER X

(1) *I, Paul, personally exhort you by the meekness and magnanimity of Christ, I who am so 'humble' before you, but who from afar show myself as 'arrogant' in your eyes* . . . (2) *I beg you not to behave in such a way that, when present with you, I should have to expend the energy which I expect to show towards certain people who think that my conduct is inspired by fleshly considerations.* (3) *For though we live in the flesh, we do not fight according to the flesh.* (4) *Indeed, our weapons of war are*

When the curtain rises in **10**, we are immediately aware of a complete change of scene. Titus and the Macedonians have disappeared, along with the collection-plates. The Apostle, himself alone before the Church, is playing a very different rôle. He is no longer the father reconciled with his children, giving them advice full of benevolence, but an irritated chief, who is defending himself by attacking his opponents. If the tone of **10^{1a}** is still quite conciliatory, it rises before the end of **10^{1b}** to become frankly sarcastic.

10$^{1-3}$ '*Autos egō Paulos.*' Paul is *alone*, speaking about authority. If later we meet the first person plural, we may be sure that it is the plural of authorship or even of authority. The author begins by exhorting his correspondents 'in the name of the humility ("*praütēs*") and the magnanimity ("*epieikeia*") of Christ,' but follows by mentioning evil accusations against himself, and the content of the exhortations is given only in **10^2**.

Of what is he accused? He must have shown himself '*tapeinos*' = lit. 'humble', here in the bad sense of 'obsequious', in the presence of the Corinthians, only to give proof of boldness, not to say insolence ('*tharrō*'), when he was at a distance, i.e. in his letter or letters. This grievance was perhaps not without apparent foundation. For does not the Apostle declare in 1 Corinthians 2^3 that he had presented himself at Corinth in a pronounced state of 'weakness, fear and trembling'? It was possible therefore to ascribe to his character what was primarily a reflection of his illness and fatigue; furthermore, it goes without saying that for him, dictating a letter required less effort than preaching. From **10^2** he expresses himself as if his visit were imminent.[1] This is why he repeats the expression 'to be bold' ('*tharrēsai*') in view of his imminent appearance.

10^2 The construction of this verse is rather complicated. The words from '*tē pepoithēsei*' to '*tolmēsai*' seem superfluous, and it is sur-

---

[1] There is a divergence at least in respect of **1–8** if not of **9**.

not of the flesh, but powerful through God to destroy fortresses. [With them] we can bring to nothing sophistries (5) and all haughty powers which array themselves against the knowledge of God, and we take prisoner all thoughts, to subject them to Christ. (6) And so we are ready to punish any disobedience, at the time when your obedience must be perfect. (7) Look at the evidence before you: if anyone boasts of

prising that no exegete has been bold enough to omit them. We shall follow this example, in view of their attestation by all the witnesses.

It must be believed that *'pepoithēsis'* here means the 'authority' (apostolic, without doubt) on which Paul wishes to draw (*'pepoith-ēsei'* = *dativus commodi*, to go with *'tharrēsai'*) and also use in justifying the decision (*'logizomai'*) to be bold (*'tolmēsai'*). He hopes however that the Corinthians will conduct themselves reasonably enough to make this attitude pointless.—The end of 10^2 and 10^3 introduces a fresh accusation against the Apostle, which is a veritable calumny: he is treated as a man living 'according to the flesh,' that is one using means suggested by worldly wisdom.

10^{4-6} develops the comparison of missionary work with a military enterprise (*'strateia'*).[2] The Apostle's weapons are 'strong through God' (*'dunata tō theō'*), efficient enough to take the entrenched positions (*'ochurōmata'*) of the enemies. Then the image is abandoned and the enemy openly named: the *'logismoi'*, the 'reasonings' of worldly wisdom (1 Cor 2^5 'wisdom of men'). Then the metaphorical language returns. A redoubt (*'hupsōma'* = lit. a 'fortified vantage point'), is spoken of as standing against the knowledge of God; this too will be taken by the weapons of the spirit. This expression makes us think of the pride of man or of the devil. In any event the scene broadens: no longer is there merely a question of calumniators, but of all the obstacles which the Apostle's preaching must overcome. The crowning glory of the victorious campaign will be the many prisoners won for Christianity, prisoners represented by *'pan noēma,'* lit. 'all thoughts,'[3] that is, the intellectual culture of the time, which must not be destroyed, but turned to the service of Christianity—an idea later very competently developed by the Apologists and especially Clement of Alexandria.

But (10^6) rebels are to be treated with severity (*'ekdikēsai'* = 'punish',[4] *'parakoē'* = 'disobedience'). This remark concerns the

---

[2] This is a favourite theme of the Apostle's, cf. Philippians 1^{30}; Colossians 2^1; Ephesians 6^{11ff}; 1 Thessalonians 2^2; 2 Timothy 4^7; and here 6^7.

[3] In N.T. language, the distinction of classical Greek between the singular *'pas'* without the article and the plural *'pantes'* with the article is no longer made. This must be taken into account in translation.

According to the Odes of Solomon 10^3, the Saviour himself makes prisoners of souls and of the world.

[4] The word *'ekdikos'* will be used elsewhere (Rom 13^4) for the armed man whom no government can do without.

belonging to Christ, let him, by his own judgement,—and I repeat—let
him take account of this: as he is Christ's, so are we. (8) *And even if I*
were to make a little too much of our authority, which the Lord has
given [us] *for your edification and not for your ruin, I should have no*

Corinthians particularly. The nature of the punishment is not speci-
fied; it was to depend on circumstances. We know that in certain
cases (cf. 1 Cor 5⁵) the Apostle did not hesitate to resort to a kind of
excommunication.

What is difficult is the connection of v. 6b (from *'hotan'* onwards)
to v. 6a. Why must punishment intervene, when (*'hotan'*) the submission of the Corinthians will be complete (*'plērōthē'*)? One could
presume it to be rather superfluous at this moment. All kinds of
rather laboured explanations have been advanced. Windisch thinks
that *'ekdikēsis'* looks towards the continuation of the campaign
beyond Corinth, a campaign by which the Apostle is to 'punish' the
pagan enemy. This is unacceptable to us both by the context and by
Paul's own conception of his mission. Others (Lietzmann, Allo) do
not seem to have noticed the problem.⁵ We think that the only way
out of the difficulty is to give up a long-standing prejudice, namely, the
belief that all aorists (here: *'plērōthē'*) must have a preterite or a future
anterior sense. Once more this tense seems to have an ingressive
sense.⁶ 'When the time comes to make your submission effective and
perfect, then *"ekdikēsis"* will intervene, if there is reason.'

10⁷ In the first clause the verb *'blepete'* can be taken as an indicative
(= 'you see'; Plummer, B.d.Cent.), or an imperative (= 'see';
Vulgate, Bachmann, Allo, Loisy, Windisch, Osty, Moffatt), or again
as an interrogative (= 'do you see?'; Synodale Version, G. Godet,
Fenton).⁷ In the first case, the sentence would mean: you see only
what is before your face (colloquially: you cannot see further than the
end of your nose). But then the new exhortations poured out in v. 7b
should be introduced by a 'but' (*'alla'* or *'alla gar'*). An analogous
remark could be made about the third interpretation. So we find the
second preferable: 'see what is before you,' that is, what is patently
obvious. The targets of v. 7b (*'ei tis'* = 'if anyone,' that is 'all those
who') are precisely those at whom the imperative *'blepete'* is aimed.
What is 'staring you in the face' is that Paul also belongs to Christ
(*'houtos kai hēmeis'*), and not only the one who boasts of so doing

⁵ F. FENTON translates *'hotan'* by 'so that,' which is ingenious but inadmissible.
⁶ Cf. BLASS–DEBRUNNER, § 331, p. 171. See also the ingressive use of the aorist
participle in Hebrews 2¹⁰ (*'agagonta'*), also in Philippians 2⁷⁻⁸ (*'labōn'*, *'geno-
menos'*); the subjunctive *'kampsē'* (*ibid.* v. 10) would also have an ingressive
sense, if that verse was meant to speak of an event which occurred following the
time of the resurrection of Christ, as certain expositors accept.
⁷ Similarly J. H. KENNEDY, *The Second and Third Epistle of S. Paul to the
Corinthians*, 1900, translates it, 'Do you look on things after the outward appearance?' *ad loc.*

reason to be ashamed, (9) in order not to seem simply to wish to intimi-
date you by my letters. (10) For 'the letters,' someone says, 'are weighty
and strong, but when he is present he lacks impressiveness and his word
lacks force.' (11) Such a one will have to realise that our actions when
present will match the words of our letters written in our absence. (12a)

(*'pepoithen heautō'* = 'he believes himself') with a touch of pride.[8]
Who are these supposedly true Christians? The 'Christ party' of 1
Corinthians 1[12]? But the existence of this party is doubtful.[9] Christians who had perhaps known Christ 'in the flesh' and to whom 5[16]
may allude? This is possible; but was there in Corinth an appreciable
number of witnesses of the early days? The reference may rather be to
Gnostics who spurned the apostolic authority under the pretext of
being inspired by Christ.

This interpretation seems to be confirmed by 10[8], which defends
just this authority (*'exousia'*), whose primary aim is edification and
not destruction.[10] He declares that if he insists on it a little too much
(*'perissoteron ti'*) he will have no reason to regret it (*'ouk aischunthēsomai'*), because his claim will not be belied by his appearance in
Corinth.

But how is the transition from 10[8] to 10[9] to be understood? How
can the absence of shame (*'ouk aischunthēsomai'*) have the consequence
or purpose (*'hina'*) of not frightening the flock (*'mē ekphobein'*)?
Earlier commentators as well as the Vulgate and Loisy attach 10[9] to
10[11] (and make a parenthesis of v. 10). In that case, a full stop must
be inserted before *'hina'* (beginning of v. 9) and the explanation must
be 'in order not to frighten anyone, I say: let that man take notice,
etc.' (beginning of v. 11). But it seems to us that then this v. 9 should
be linked to v. 8 by a *'de'* or a *'kai'*. Windisch is of the opinion that a
few words have been lost; but this is a 'solution of despair.' We consider that Bachmann puts us on the right track. He retains the comma
between v. 8 and v. 9, but interpolates the adverb 'only' before
'ekphobein' in v. 9; this is perfectly legitimate.[11] Paul does not wish to
appear as one who strikes the empty air, simply 'to inspire fear.' The

---

[8] Cf. the *'pepoithotes eph' heautois'* of Luke 18[9].—Also *'eph' heautou'* (v. 7) seems
to mean, 'if anyone believes himself enlightened, he should be clear-sighted
enough to see for himself what is right in front of his eyes.'
[9] See our Commentary on 1 Corinthians *ad loc.*
[10] How could Paul have 'destroyed' (*'kathairesis'*)? It is probably an allusion to
those who wished to destroy his work. Paul does not act like them. And so he takes
care to do his own building (*'oikodomē'*), instead of introducing himself into
Churches built by others. Another explanation, which seems less probable but
which remains possible, supposes that Paul could have 'destroyed' by abusing his
authority.
[11] It is known that this restriction is not always expressed in Greek; thus Luther
was perfectly right to speak of *sola fide* in Romans 3[28], although *sola* is not found
in the text.

Assuredly we do not wish to risk comparison or competition with certain persons who push themselves forward. (12b) *But by measuring ourselves by our own measure, and by comparing ourselves [solely] with ourselves, (13) we shall not go beyond the limit in pushing ourselves forward. On the contrary, we shall measure with the rule which God [Himself] gave us, by allowing us to reach you. (14) For we do not overstretch ourselves, which would be the case if we had not come among you. Indeed we were the first to bring you the gospel of Christ.*

particle '*hōsan*' = 'as it were' seems to confirm this interpretation.[12]

A similar thing occurs in **10¹⁰**, in which the Apostle is accused of a purely verbal severity; his letters are strong ('*ischurai*') and even weighty, that is hard to bear ('*bareiai*'[13]), but as for his personal presence, what a disappointment! He is weak ('*asthenēs*') and his speaking lamentable ('*exouthenēmenos*').[14]

In **10¹¹** the Apostle denies these accusations emphatically. 'The preacher and the giver of orders will not be different from the letter-writer'; '*tō ergō*' = 'in the act.'

10¹²⁻¹³ A new piece of self-justification. Paul remarks, a little caustically, that he does not wish to compare himself to those who 'blow their own trumpets' ('*heautous sunistanontes*'), that is those whom we know slightly through the polemical passage **4¹¹⁻¹²**.

The text of **10¹²** and the beginning of **10¹³** has come down to us in two forms: the longer, adopted by Nestlé, is favoured by the majority of witnesses. It appears to mean: 'they are people who measure themselves by their own standard, for they are stupid ('*ou suniasin*'). But what the author seems to hold against them is, on the contrary, the placing of themselves above others and notably above the Apostle. The short reading[15] which omits the four words '*ou suniasin hēmeis de*' seems to us to make better sense. Then v. 12 is already speaking about Paul: we compare ourselves only to ourselves, that is, 'we judge ourselves in the light of the ideal which we have set before ourselves, or rather the one which God sets before us' (v. 13 from '*hou emerisen hēmin ho theos*'). 'We make no outrageous boast' ('*eis ta ametra*').

---

[12] BLASS–DEBRUNNER, § 453 note (3): '*hōsan*' = 'so to speak.'
[13] Not to be translated as 'serious.'
[14] Cf. once more 1 Corinthians 2³—'*exoutheneō*' or '*exoudeneō*' lit. = 'to despise'.—Perhaps his standing as a craftsman also made a bad impression: 'He is not an intellectual,' the Greeks may have said. Evidently the Jews were much more appreciative of the value of manual work; on this point see the instructive publication by W. BIENERT, *Die Arbeit nach der Lehre der Bibel* (Stuttgart 1954), who compares Jewish and Greek ideas on this subject; cf. our review of this work in *RHPR* 1956, pp. 83ff.
[15] Given by the principal witnesses of the so-called Western text, i.e. D, it (vg), and the Vulgate.

(15) *And so we do not boast disproportionately,* [*as would be the case if we were taking advantage*] *of the work of others. But we hope with the strengthening of your faith to see our work extend among you—* [*always*] *within the limits of our measure.* (16) *And an increase of support will allow us to carry the gospel beyond your frontiers.* [*And saying this*] *we do not wish to boast by looking towards ground already prepared by others, according to the measure which has been given to them.* (17) '*If any one boasts, let him boast in the Lord!*' (18) *For it is not the man who sings his own praises who is approved, but he who is commended by the Lord.*

10^{13} is therefore, in this text, the normal continuation of 10^{12}. Detailed explanation of 10^{13} presents new difficulties, however. The expression '*metron tou kanonos*' = 'the measure of the rule' (?) is not very clear. The B.d.Cent. translates 'within the limits of the province;' similarly Plummer ('limit of that sphere'); the Synodale Version, 'in the limits of the portion which God has assigned to us.' But '*kanōn*' does not mean either 'province' or 'sphere' or 'portion'. The only way out of the difficulties is to attach '*hou*' to '*metron*' and not to '*kanonos*', and to take '*kanonos*' as a genitive of quality. The 'measure' is that established by a 'standard' (that is the sense of '*kanōn*') set by God against the Apostle. Immediately the repetition of '*metron*' near the end of 10^{13} is made clear.[16] It is as if the author had wished—without success, however—to prevent exegetes from attaching '*hou*' to '*kanonos*'! In accordance with this programme Paul evangelised the heathen, and more particularly those who had not yet been reached by the preaching of other Christian missionaries. This is underlined by the end of v. 13 as well as vv. 14 and 15.

He has arrived: he has gone as far as Corinth ('*ephikesthai*', etc., end of v. 13), and before the others. He has not overreached himself ('*ou huperekteinomen heatous*'), v. 14, as would have been the case if he had not succeeded in reaching Corinth ('*hos mē ephiknoumenoi*'), and before the others ('*ephthasamen*').[17]

10^{15} He cannot then be reproached with taking advantage of work performed by others ('*en allotriois kopois*'), in order to boast unfairly ('*eis ta ametra*' = lit. 'in a way which would go beyond the measure').

10^{15b}, from '*elpida*' = 'hope', must be taken closely with v. 16. The author expresses the hope that, firstly, the faith of the Corinthians will increase further ('*auxanomenēs tēs pisteōs humōn*'), and secondly

---

[16] We admit that the 'attraction' of the relative, into the genitive, is not altogether correct in our explanation. But the nearness of '*kanonos*' was sufficient to give rise to it.
[17] Instead of '*huperekteinomen*' it would be preferable to read '*huperekteinamen*' = 'we have not overstretched', etc. But no witness supports this variant. The present tense is also justified, however.

'grow' or 'spread' further in Greece (*'megalunthēnai'*),[18] in accordance with his programme (*'kata ton kanona hēmōn'*), in order to overflow (*'eis perisseian'*). What does this mean? It is made clear by what follows (v. 16a).[19] (*'Eis perisseian'* should be attached to v. 16.)

He hopes to carry the good news further (*'ta huperekeina humōn'*) and makes it clear that he will sow only on virgin soil (*'ouk en allotriō kanoni'* = lit. 'without trespassing on someone else's preserves.' His ideal is to be the first to plant the flag.

Detailed explanation of **10[16b]** does however present some difficulty. If *'eis'* is taken with *'ta huperekeina,'* how is the bare infinitive *'euanggelizesthai'* = 'to evangelise' to be reconciled with what precedes?[20] Windisch even finds the construction 'intolerable' (*'unerträglich'*, p. 313). We propose to leave the infinitive with its indispensable preposition (*'eis'*) and to take *'ta huperekaina'* = 'the regions beyond you' without *'eis'*, as the direct object of *'euanggelisasthai'* taken as transitive.[21] (See our translation.)

What is more troublesome is how to understand the sense of *'ta hetoima'* in v. 16b. It is usually rendered as 'on ground already prepared,' namely by others. But *'hetoimos'*, even when its sense is passive, always signifies prepared 'for someone' or 'for something.' We can see only one way of cutting a passage through this thicket, and that is to attach the wretched *'eis to hetoima'* to *'en allotriō kanoni'*: there is for each a rule, in view of what is prepared for him, i.e. which fixes what God destines for him. It is then a question of not boasting about what God has statutorily reserved for others.[22]

10[17–18] raises us at a stroke to the heights of fundamental truths, **10[17]** being a summary of Jeremiah 9[22–3].[23] **10[18]** gives the conclusion by re-introducing the idea developed in v. 12. It is not a question of

---

[18] It is sometimes explained that *'megalunthēnai'* refers to Paul's work in Corinth (the interpretation taken for instance by the Synodale Version), but the interpretation which we have adopted and which is also used by Crampon and the B.d.Cent. fits better with v. 16. *'Megalunthēnai'* has of course a touch of metonomy: it is Paul's work which will spread.

[19] What is the meaning of *'en humin'* (v. 15)? The following words show that it is not about the work in Corinth. *'En humin'* signifies 'among you Greeks,' or 'in Greece.'

[20] An attempt could be made to consider this infinitive as following after *'megalunthēnai'*. But then we could expect to find the two infinitives joined by *'kai'*.

[21] This usage is attested by Galatians 1[9] and 1 Peter 1[12] and by other passages in the Epistle to the Hebrews, St. Luke's Gospel, the Acts and Revelation.

[22] We do not claim our interpretation to be absolutely satisfying; but it seems to us to be less impossible than the others.

[23] 'Let not the wise man glory in his wisdom ... but let him who glories glory in this, that he understands and knows me.'

S.E.C.—7

commending oneself. One is '*dokimos*' = 'approved', 'fit for service' only if one is established by God.[24] It must be confessed that after the sections of apologetic written in a rather tortured style,[25] there is something rather comforting in the sober and dignified conclusion of vv. 17 and 18.

[24] There is a slight play on words, since '*sunistanō*' signifies both 'to establish' and 'to commend.'

[25] The incoherences of style in the passage 10^{11-16}, which Windisch finds 'notably clumsy,' containing 'oddly confused expressions' must not be exaggerated.— Lietzmann even speaks of 'chopped up pieces of sentences, violently thrown together.'

CHAPTER XI

(1) *Ah! would that you could put up with a small sample of my foolishness! Do, indeed, put up with it from me.* (2) *For I feel for you a burning religious affection. Indeed, I betrothed you to one husband, Christ, like a pure virgin.* (3) *But I am afraid that as Eve was led astray by the trickery of the serpent your minds may be misled into abandoning their*

In **11** the Apostle continues, rather more forcefully still, his self-defence against those who belittle his work and contest the authenticity of his apostleship. The permanent value of this continuation lies, in the first place, in the elements of a phenomenological description of true apostleship which it presents to us—authentic apostleship will perform miracles, it is selfless, without pride, speaks no evil, does not trespass on the ground where others are working. And secondly, this chapter provides some unpublished details about Paul's life.

Who are the 'transcendent Apostles' (*'huperlian*[1] *apostoloi'*), as the author ironically terms them? It is difficult not to think of the brothers of Jesus and of the Twelve, who in the eyes of certain Jewish-Christian missionaries were the only ones who mattered, which does not absolutely prove that they themselves belittled Paul's work.[2]

We may follow Windisch and subdivide this essay in apologetics into several sections:

(a) **11**[1-4] Introduction. The author asks the Corinthians to bear with a little folly from him.

(b) **11**[5-15] Paul insists on the selfless nature of his apostleship.

(c) **11**[16-21a] is an introduction to the next section, and also resumes the theme of (a).

(d) **11**[21b-33] Paul's Jewish descent and catalogues of 'peristases'. The style approaches that of poetic prose.

(e) **12**[1-10] Personal revelations granted by God.

(f) **12**[11-13] Conclusion.

11[1-4] V.1a sets down the request which is the object of this passage (see above). '*Ōphelon*',[3] second aorist of '*opheilō*', is a stereotyped form which in general introduces the statement of a wish considered

---

[1] '*Huperlian*' = 'beyond all measure' should not simply indicate a higher grade, but something which defies any comparison. That is why the rendering 'arch-apostles' seems to us to be too weak.

[2] On the relationships of Paul with the Jerusalem Apostles, cf. M. GOGUEL, *The Birth of Christianity*, ET London 1953, pp. 292ff.

[3] Certain witnesses read '*ophelon*' (same sense).

simple directness with regard to Christ. (4) Indeed, let another come announcing another Jesus, whom we had not announced, or another Spirit which you had not received, or another gospel which you had not embraced, and you subscribe to it very readily. (5) Now I claim to

as unrealisable (cf. the Latin '*utinam*' with imperfect subjunctive—in English 'O that,' 'would that', etc.). This is not so here, but the author undoubtedly wished to stress the strange nature of his request.— Should the pronoun '*mou*' at the beginning of **11¹** be taken with '*aneichesthe*' = 'that you should bear with me,' or with '*aphrosunēs*' = 'bear my folly'? In spite of the expression '*anechesthe mou*' at the end of the verse, it seems to us that the second is the correct explication. For otherwise, there would be nothing to attach the genitive '*aphrosunēs*'[4] to. '*Aphrosunē*'[5] = 'madness' is of course in antithesis to '*sophia*' = 'wisdom'.

The Apostle 'plays the madman' in order to say certain truths which in normal circumstances he would discreetly keep to himself.[6]

11² '*Zēlō*' perhaps = 'I am jealous' (in the strong sense, conjugal); yet later it is not the Apostle, but Christ who is presented as the betrothed of the Church; '*zēlō*' should then signify: 'to watch over someone with religious zeal.' The Apostle seems to speak of himself as the father of the Church in Corinth, which he presents ('*parastēsai*') to Christ. He has prepared it as a holy virgin ('*parthenos hagnēn*') intended for one husband only ('*heni andri*': there are not two gospels, see **11⁴** and Galatians 1⁶⁻⁹).

11³ The Church which might be unfaithful, is comparable to Eve led astray by the serpent (Gen 3), a not very pertinent comparison, because she did not exactly betray her husband.[7] '*Panourgia*' (cf. **12¹⁶** '*pan-ourgos*') indicates an extreme *malignity* which is capable of anything ('*pan ergon*').[8] The serpent is probably identified with the

---

[4] We have a right to look on '*aneichesthe*' as an imperfect indicative and not an imperative (despite the Synodale Version), whilst '*anechesthe*' at the end of the verse is evidently an imperative. '*Alla kai*' before this imperative seems to signify 'I am not content with expressing a wish, I beseech you . . .'. Sic BLASS–DEBRUNNER § 448, note 6. One could venture to construe '*aneichesthe mikron ti mou*,' but the construction '*anechesthai ti tinos*' (bear with something for somebody) seems very rare.

[5] Why does the Apostle not use for 'madness' the term '*mōria*'? Undoubtedly because he uses it as a technical term to indicate Christian madness, of which there is no question here (cf. 1 Cor 1¹⁸⁻²⁵).

[6] The case of Solon, who pretended madness in order to preach truths which were frowned on, is therefore not a complete parallel. The Athenian legislator was motivated by prudence.

[7] Another lesson is drawn from Eve's fall in 1 Timothy 2¹³⁻¹⁵.

[8] The fall is therefore the result of deceit, something which ought never to have happened, and not (as certain theosophists claim) mere withdrawal from 'the divine sphere,' due to the necessities of 'human evolution'!

*have been in no way inferior to the 'transcendent' apostles. (6) And
even though in eloquence I am only an ordinary man, the same thing
cannot be said about my knowledge, and this we have shown you, at
every opportunity, and in every respect. (7) Or could I have committed a
sin because, by humbling myself to raise you up, I announced the gospel
of God to you without payment? (8) I plundered other churches by
accepting the means of livelihood [from them] in order to serve you.
(9) And when I arrived among you, even though I was in need, I was a
burden to no one. It was the brethren who came from Macedonia who
filled the gap in my resources. And I absolutely refrained from being a
burden on you, and I shall [continue to] refrain. (10) As true as is the
Christian truth in me, no one will be able to close my mouth if I boast
thus in the regions of Greece. (11) Why? Because I do not love you?
God knows that I do. (12) What I do, I will continue to do, in order to
put an end to any pretext used by those who seek pretexts in order to
pass as our equals on the point about which they boast. (13) For these*

devil, in accordance with a Jewish tradition which is also found in
Revelation 12⁹ and 20². In any case it prefigures the false brethren
here.

11⁴ Here they are. They preach 'another Jesus,' doubtless a reference
to a Christology which viewed the person and life of Jesus from too
earthly an angle, as the Ebionites did later. In this instance the false
gospel was that which sought to impose the Mosaic Law on the
Greeks. It is difficult to understand what the author means by 'another Holy Spirit.' It may be the idea known through the Gospel
according to the Hebrews, in which the Spirit is the mother of Jesus.[9]
The expression *'pneuma heteron lambanete'* = 'you accept another
spirit' suggests the belief that the Corinthians really do accept doc-
trines of this kind. But there may be some exaggeration involved.[10]

11⁵⁻¹⁵. 11⁵ The *'huperlian apostoloi,'* the 'transcendent apostles,' as we
have already said, can hardly be other than those at Jerusalem. Did
they do missionary work themselves and disturb Paul's congrega-

---

[9] 'Then my mother the Holy Spirit seized me by one of my hairs and carried me
away to the great Mount Tabor' (*'arti elabe me hē mētēr mou to hagion pneuma en
mia tōn trichōn mou, kai apēnegke me eis to oros to mega thabōr'*). ORIGEN,
Commentary on John, vol. II, 12, § 87, ed. Preuschen, *GCS* p. 67.—It should be
borne in mind that in Hebrew the spirit *'ruah'* is feminine. This concept evidently
brings us close to the pagan triads: father-mother-son, and has nothing in common
with the Christology of Paul and John.

[10] Moreover, we will not vouch for the authenticity of the word *'lambanete'*,
although, unless we are mistaken, it is attested by all the witnesses. For it is redundant and upsets the construction. By omitting it, a well-balanced sentence is
obtained: 'If any preach another Jesus whom we had not preached, or another
Spirit which you had not accepted, or another gospel which you had not received,
you put up with it splendidly.' The thought would also be more in keeping with
the context, which speaks solely of what the Corinthians can *bear* (cf. v. 1). So
they are not being reproached for having already *accepted* any false teaching.

unhappy people are false apostles, deceitful workmen, who disguise
themselves as apostles of Christ. (14) *There is nothing surprising in that,*
for even Satan disguises himself as an angel of light. (15) *So it is not to*
be wondered at if his servants disguise themselves as servants of right-
eousness. But their end will be worthy of their works. (16) *I repeat: let*

tions? Except for Peter, we have no information whatever about
missionary work by the Twelve in pagan lands.

But according to 1 Corinthians 9[5] the brothers of Jesus made
missionary journeys, and we know that they were great 'Judaisers', at
least in the case of James.[11] Did they perhaps go to Corinth? It is not
impossible, though they were certainly not the 'first comers' ('*ho*
erchomenos', v. 4). The more probable answer is that they may have
been some emissaries from Jerusalem who swore by the Twelve (cf.
the '*tines apo Iakōbou*,' Gal 2[2]).[12]

11[6] '*Idiōtēs*' has a bad sense here; commonly the sense is 'uninstruct-
ed'. The Apostle admits his lack of rhetorical eloquence if placed
alongside the Greeks. But he claims the possession of knowledge
('*gnōsis*') which he teaches clearly and without reserve ('*en panti*
phanerōsantes,' '*autēn*' being understood).

11[7] Here the sarcastic tone, attenuated earlier, is even more forceful.
Was it a sin to bring the gospel without fee? Not altogether a pointless question, since according to 1 Corinthians 9[1-18] even this self-
lessness had provided weapons for those who belittled his apostleship.

8[8-11] The Apostle recalls that if in distress he accepted money from the
Churches in Macedonia,[13] it was done so as not to be a burden on the
Corinthians. It was undoubtedly because of his particularly cordial
and happy relationship with the Macedonians that he consented, in
their case, to make an exception to his rule of earning his living by
working as weaver or tent-maker (Acts 18[13]).

He even declares (v. 8) that he 'robbed' ('*esulēsa*') other Churches.
This is certainly the very expression used by the evil-minded opponents who accused him of living at Corinthian expense.—The sub-
sidies ('*opsōnion*') intended to 'cancel his deficit' had been brought by
messengers from Macedonia ('*to husterēma mou eplērōsan*,' etc.).—

---

[11] See *infra* the Appendix on apostleship.
[12] In a certain type of Judaeo-Christianity which can be found in the Pseudo-
Clementine writings, hatred of Paul seems to have persisted for quite a long time,
and sometimes he seems to be the target in the likeness of Simon Magus. Cf.
O. CULLMANN, 'Le problème littéraire et historique du roman pseudo-clémentin,'
EHPR 23, Paris 1930, pp. 243–50.
[13] In the case of Philippi this point is explicitly confirmed in Philippians
4 [10,15].

*no one take me for a madman: or else leave me to play the fool, so that
in my turn, I can boast a little!* (17) *What I say, I do not say as a Christian, but as one in a paroxysm of madness, by placing myself on that
ground which is the ground of boastfulness.* (18) *At a time when so*

'*Abarēs*' = 'weightless', 'not a burden to.' '*Phrattein*' or '*sphrattein*'
= 'to close an opening,' especially an insolent or dangerous mouth.
Cf. Romans 3[19] and Hebrews 11[33]. The end of v. 11 means: God
knows *that it is so*.

11[12] The calumnies must be ended. But what is the meaning of the
expression '*en hō kauchōntai*' = 'in what they boast'? '*En hō*' could
have a temporal or adversative sense: 'while' or 'whilst' (B.d.Cent.).
But it is perhaps rather as an indication of intensity that it is intended:
'the more they boast,'[14] the more obvious it will be that they are no
better than ourselves ('*heurethōsin kathōs kai hēmeis*').

11[13–15] complete the portrait of the opponents with some very serious
accusations, which they must have taken as insults. (a) They are false
apostles (cf. **11**[4]), who disguise the truth. (b) They are deceivers ('*dol-
ioi*'), undoubtedly because they use calumny and other ungenerous
methods, in order to gain possession of the congregation. The Apostle
does not even apply to them the criteria of specifically Christian
ethics (love, patience, humility); he judges them by the standard of a
common elementary ethic. (c) They are servants of Satan ('*diakonoi
autou*', v. 15), disguised as servants of the righteous cause ('*diakonoi
dikaiosunēs*'). This passage supposes, moreover, a curious habit of
Satan himself: he knows how to camouflage himself as an angel of
light, the better to lead men astray. There is no text on this point in
the Old Testament. But the idea is developed in the 'Life of Adam
and Eve.'[15]

Like Satan himself, his servants disguise themselves. The assimilation of false brethren into instruments of Satan adds up to an enor-
mous accusation. It may be asked, therefore, whether the Apostle
Paul had no other more precise complaints of a moral nature against
them, and **11**[20] confirms this expectation. Nevertheless it must be
borne in mind also that accusations of this type formed part of the
arsenal of invective of early apologetics; see for this the Epistle of
Jude.

[14] Others (Allo, Osty) think that '*en hō*' indicates the object or the relation of
the boasting. But what is this relation?
[15] See § 10f. 'Then Satan became angry and assumed the shining form of the
angels'; then he engages in a discussion with Eve. Cf. KAUTZSCH, *Pseudepigraphen*, p. 513, CHARLES, *Pseudepigrapha*, p. 136.—For analogous accounts
among the Hindus, cf. RICHARD GARBE, *Indien und das Christentum*, 1914, p. 111.
—According to the Theosophists (Adyar ritual), disturbing beings sometimes
assume a very good likeness of the (supernatural) Master, who is guiding a
disciple. But they do not succeed in counterfeiting his look. Cf. LEADBEATER,
L'occultisme dans la nature I, 2nd edn 1926, pp. 41ff.

*many [others] boast of purely human prerogatives, I will boast also.
(19) For you gladly bear with madmen, you who are wise.* (20) *You
bear with those who enslave you, who devour you, who lay hands upon
you, who treat you with arrogance, who strike you in the face.* (21) *I
say it to your shame; for we have, apparently, shown ourselves too
weak. But whatever qualification may be advanced—I speak as a madman—I can advance it also.* (22) *They are Hebrews? So am I. Israelites? So am I. Descendants of Abraham? So am I.* (23) *Ministers of
Christ?—I speak as one raving— I am more one than they. I have had
to bear many more hardships than they, many more imprisonments,
beatings innumerable, often I was at death's door.*

11¹⁵ᵇ '*Hōn to telos*' = 'their end,' etc., gives voice to a threat or
sinister prophecy which is made particularly impressive by its terse-
ness.

11¹⁶⁻²¹ Introduction to the second part of the 'foolish discourse.' The
apology of unreason is nearly the same as in the passage **11¹⁻⁶**, without the utterance of any new accusations against his opponents.

Some difficulties of detail. What is the exact meaning of '*dexasthe
me hōs aphrona*'? 'Accept me although I am mad'? or 'take me as
mad'?[16] The first interpretation seems the better; for the Apostle
wishes, before continuing, to gain the full attention of the recipients.
The beginning of v. 16, however, recalls that the author is not really
mad.

11¹⁷ '*En tautē tē hupostasei*' = 'with this assurance'(?) is difficult.[17] As
in **9⁴**, it seems that '*hupostasis*' should mean 'confidence', and it is
usually translated thus; then the sense would be: 'the confidence with
which I boast is a proof of my madness.' Weizsäcker[18] on the other
hand translates '*hupostasis*' by '*Standpunkt*' = by putting myself at
the point of view of him who boasts. This sense would be suitable,
but is poorly attested. After due consideration we think that once
more there is good reason to take the basic sense as imposed by ety-
mology: '*hupostasis*' is a 'sup-position' or 'hypo-thesis', the *supposition* is that Paul is really boasting, thanks to a fit of madness.[19] (Cf.
9⁵ for this sense of '*hupostasis*'.)

11¹⁸⁻²⁰ present no particular problems; they provide additional information about the mentality and behaviour of the false apostles. They
are thirsting for power ('*katadouloi*', '*lambanei*'), proud ('*epairetai*'),[20]

[16] *Sic* Fenton, Plummer. *Aliter* Bachmann.
[17] Windisch observes that it is very difficult to understand because '*hupostasis*'
has several senses, none of which is suitable here.
[18] *Das Neue Testament*, Tübingen 1904.
[19] It is to G. GODET'S credit to have put forward this translation; see p. 289 of
his *Commentaire*.
[20] The B.d.Cent. translates '*epairomai*' by 'treat with insolence'; then something like '*huper humōn*' would have to be understood.

full of self-interest (*'katesthiei'*), ill-behaved (*'eis prosōpon humas derei,'* lit. = 'he strikes you'). Also to be noted is the irony with which the author treats as 'reasonable' (*'phronimoi'*) his detractors, who support people who are more abnormal than the Apostle himself (*'anechesthe tōn aphronōn phronimoi ontes'*).

11²¹ *'Atimia'* = 'shame'. Who should be ashamed? The Corinthians or the Apostle? Each of these interpretations can be upheld: the Corinthians should be ashamed of taking the Apostle's kindness as weakness (Chrysostom, Calvin, G. Godet, Lietzmann). But the Apostle could also be ashamed of a real weakness (*sic* the majority of expositors).²¹ — *'Hōs hoti'*²² has the same sense as *'hōs'* with a participle: 'as if' we were weak.

11²²⁻³³ The second foolish discourse, **11²¹ᵇ⁻³³** (Windisch: 'the second stage of the foolish discourse'). It can be subdivided into four strophes: **11²²⁻²³; 11²⁴⁻²⁵; 11²⁶; 11²⁷⁻²⁹**.

11²² contains nothing extraordinary, however. The Apostle is a Hebrew in language,²³ an Israelite in religion,²⁴ a descendant of Abraham by race.²⁵

11²³ begins to give some signs of 'madness' (*'paraphronōn'* = 'reasoning faultily, in an unhealthy way,' 'running off the rails'). The author boasts of having served the Lord better than the others (*'huper egō'*),²⁶ of having undergone a vast quantity of hardships and imprisonments (*'perissoterōs'*), of having been beaten beyond all reason (*'huperballontōs'*).²⁷—*'Thanatoi'* = 'mortal dangers'.²⁸

²¹ Osty leaves the choice open. So do we.
²² Cf. BLASS–DEBRUNNER § 396.
²³ He did not forget this as did many Jews of the dispersion, Philo for example.
—Moreover, it was possible to embrace the Israelite religion without being Jewish (proselytes, and later the Karaïtes in the Crimea).—Philippians 3⁵ gives the further information that the Apostle was of the tribe of Benjamin, like his namesake, the king of Israel, whom he resembles a little in fierceness of temperament and tragic greatness of destiny.—On the sense of *'Hebraios'* cf. also Acts 6¹ where the Hebrews are contrasted with the Hellenists who spoke Greek. The same is meant in Philippians 3⁵ (*'Hebraios ex Hebraiōn'*). On the sense of *'Hebraios'* in Josephus, cf. WINDISCH p. 351.
²⁴ The religious sense of *'Israēlitēs'* is attested by such texts as John 1⁴⁷; Romans 9⁴; 11¹.
²⁵ According to Windisch *'sperma Abraam'* should allude primarily to the promises made to Abraham. But of course these promises are addressed only to his posterity.
²⁶ *'Huper'* without a complement has almost become an adverb = 'to a higher degree,' 'better'. Cf. BLASS–DEBRUNNER § 230.
²⁷ This is usually translated 'more than the others.' But this would weaken the expression. Indirectly we attribute an analogous sense to *'perissoterōs'*.
²⁸ According to the Israelites one is already under the empire of death when one is seized by diseases or other serious disorders. See E. JACOB, *Theology of the Old Testament*, ET London 1958, p. 301.

(24) *Five times I received the thirty-nine lashes from the Jews; (25) three times I was beaten with rods; once I was stoned; three times I have been shipwrecked, and I have spent a day and a night adrift at sea. (26) In my journeys I was often in danger from rivers, in danger from brigands in danger from the Jews, in danger from the Gentiles; in danger in town, in danger in the country, in danger on the sea, in danger by false bothers. (27) I have spent my life in labours and fatigues. Often I was deprived of sleep, I suffered hunger and thirst, often I had to go fasting and to suffer cold and destitution. (28) And apart from all the rest, I bore my daily burden: the care of all the churches.*

11^{24-27} give details of these 'peristases' of which 11^{23} had stated the 'argument'. Note that imprisonments (in the plural) are unknown, for this period, to the Acts of the Apostles, which speaks only of a gaoling in Philippi. But in any case one may add an imprisonment at Ephesus[29] (cf. 1 Corinthians 15^{31-32}).

11^{24} Here the *'plēgai'* = 'blows' of v. 23 are given in detail: five times the Apostle has received 39 lashes inflicted by the Jewish authorities. These authorities could, not only in Palestine but also in the diaspora, inflict this punishment on their adherents for offences of a religious kind among others.[30] We have no knowledge of the places where Paul received the lashes.

11^{25} The three beatings with rods (*'tris errhabdisthēn'*) must refer to punishments inflicted by non-Jewish authorities. The Acts of the Apostles gives one example in 16^{22} (Philippi). Since Paul was a Roman citizen (by birth), this punishment was illegal, as is underlined by such texts as Acts 16^{37} and 22^{25}.[31] See the Lex Julia in the

---

[29] On this matter readers are referred to G. S. DUNCAN, *St. Paul's Ephesian Ministry*, 1929, and to W. MICHAELIS: (a) 'Die Gefangenschaft des Paulus in Ephesus und das Itinerarium des Timotheos' *Neutestamentliche Forschungen*, I, 3, 1925; (b) 'Die Pastoral- und Gefangenschaftsbriefe,' *ibid.* I, 6, 1930; (c) 'Die Datierung des Philipper-Briefs,' *ibid.* I, 8, 1953. Other publications are cited by M. GOGUEL, *Introduction au Nouveau Testament*, IV, 2, pp. 426ff, and by P. BONNARD, *Commentaire de l'Epître aux Philippiens*, Neuchâtel and Paris 1950.

[30] Cf. SCHÜRER, *Geschichte des jüdischen Volkes*, 4th edn III, p. 114, and JUSTER, *Les Juifs dans l'Empire romain*, II, p. 161. The lash was a cruel punishment, which sometimes caused the death of the wrongdoer. It was administered with leather thongs, two thirds of the lashes being given across the back, one third across the chest. Details in Bab. Talmud Maccoth III, 12 (GOLDSCHMIDT IX, p. 238). Other rabbinic texts are listed by WETTSTEIN, *ad loc.* Thirty-nine lashes only were given to ensure that the regulation number of forty was not exceeded (cf. Deut 25^3). It may be added that according to the Midrash Rabba on Numbers (FREED-MANN, p. 738), the number 40 was caused by the 40 curses which were heaped, it appears, on Adam, Eve and the serpent after the Fall.

[31] The writer of this book, in his position as a paganophile, makes it clear that the authorities were unaware of his citizenship—poor comfort for the victim.

writings of the jurist Paulus, *Sententiae* V 26.1.[32]
His stoning—which happily did not have the same tragic result as
in Stephen's case, although he was left for dead—is briefly mentioned
in Acts 14[19] (Lystra), not as being ordered by synagogue authority,
but as being perpetrated by a riot engineered by the Jews.[33]
The three shipwrecks (*'tris enauagēsa'*) are not known to the Acts
of the Apostles. But a fourth took place, as we know, during the
voyage to Rome (Acts 27). In the course of one of these three dis-
asters the Apostle spent twenty-four hours (*'nuchthēmeron'*) 'in the
deep,' that is in the open sea.[34]

11[26] *'Hodoiporiai'* = 'journeys on roads,' must be in contrast with
sea-voyages. It is unnecessary to recall that even under the *pax
Romana*, certain regions notably in Asia Minor were still very back-
ward in the comfort and safety of their communications. The 'danger
from rivers' (*'kindunoi potamōn'*) must refer to the absence of bridges
or easily negotiable fords.[35] As for 'brigands', there were undoubtedly some of these in the country areas (*'erēmia'*, same verse);[36] the
dangers from Jews and from Gentiles are mentioned in Acts. The
false brethren (*'pseudadelphoi'*) are (alas!) Christians hostile to the
Pauline evangel; this may refer to the Judaisers like those opposed in

---

[32] Cf. Cicero, *in Verrem*, II, 5 (Teubner, p. 139) and Josephus, *War*, I, 14.9
(= § 308).—The *Sententiae* of PAULUS can be found in E. HUSCHKE, *Juris-
prudentiae Antejustinianae Reliquiae*, vol. 2 (Teubner series). However, the Lex
Julia forbade beating only when the Roman citizen had previously appealed to
the Emperor. This may be the reason why T. MOMMSEN, *Droit pénal romain*
(Duquesne translation, 1907, vol. V, pp. 34 and 52) prefers to bring forward a
Lex Porcia, passed, it appears, through the initiative of Cato the Elder.—One case
of beating authorised by the procurator Florus (64–6) against Jews of equestrian
rank is mentioned as an unprecedented action by JOSEPHUS, *Wars of the Jews*, II,
14.9 (= § 308).
[33] It is not true that this punishment was specifically Jewish. It is also found
among the Persians, Greeks and Romans (cf. PAULY WISSOWA, *Realenzyklopädie*,
sub. lapidatio). But among the Jews it was the obligatory punishment for certain
religious crimes, like false prophecy, blasphemy, unauthorised entry into the
sanctuary, as well as for certain cases of incest. See especially Leviticus 20;
Deuteronomy 13 and 17; Exodus 19; Deuteronomy 21 and 22. According to
Mishna Sanhedrin 6.4–5 (GOLDSCHMIDT, vol. 8, p. 642f) those who had been
stoned, women excepted, were to be subsequently hanged.
[34] THEOPHYLACT (*MPG* 124, col. 924 B) echoes a tradition according to which
the Apostle was at Lystra thrown into a well called *'buthos'* (only mentioned for
interest).—Even a strong swimmer would have difficulty in remaining afloat for
so long 'in the billows.' It must be supposed that as in the disaster recounted in
Acts 27[44], those in the shipwreck, or some of them, were able to save themselves
on pieces of floating wreckage (*'epi tinōn tōn apo tou ploiou'*); cf. G. Godet.
[35] We could easily believe in such dangers, even if the Emperor Barbarossa had
not been drowned in the Calicadnus in Cilicia in 1190, as some commentators
gravely point out.
[36] There is no question at this period of pirates who had their haunts in Cilicia.
Pompey had 'pacified' them.

(29) *Who is weak, and I am not weak also? Who stumbles, and I do
not get into a fever about it?* (30) *If there must be boasting, I shall boast
of my wretchedness.* (31) *The God and Father of our Lord Jesus Christ—
may He be blessed for ever—knows that I do not lie.*—(32) *At Damascus
the governor for King Aretas had the city of the Damascenes under
guard in order to capture me,* (33) *and I had to be let down in a basket
through a window in the city wall, and thus I escaped him.*

the Epistle to the Galatians,[37] or in a more general way to all 'mis-
chief-makers'. But the 'dangers' which they cause are put on the same
plane as those caused by brigands, the sea, etc.; we may ask therefore
whether those in question were not traitors who denounced the
Apostle to the authorities.

With **11²⁷** a new strophe in this rhythmic discourse begins. Here the
point is less about acute dangers than the sum total of the Apostle's
wretched situation which is characterized by *'kopos kai mochthos'* =
'hardship and wretchedness.' The *'nēsteiai'* are certainly not voluntary 'fasts'; the context demands the opposite. Similarly, the 'sleeplessness' (*'agrupniai'*) is sleeplessness caused by circumstances.[38] The
hunger and thirst (*'limos kai dipsos'*) are not due perhaps solely to his
poverty, but again to the lack of resources in sparsely populated
areas. The cold and destitution (*'psuchos kai gumnotēs'*) may refer to
raids by brigands.[39]

To these distresses are added (**11²⁷⁻²⁸**) the perpetual worries
(*'kath' hēmeran'*) for his Churches; *'chōris tōn parektos'* = 'the rest
apart,' that is in addition to the listed misfortunes. *'Epistasis'* may
mean 'tension'; here the sense of 'burden' is more suitable. But the
best interpretation in our opinion is that of Windisch: 'pressure', i.e.
'oppression'.[40]

11²⁹ characterises the Apostle's painful sympathy for his congrega-
tions. He suffers in their physical and moral weaknesses (*'astheneō'*);
he 'has a fever'[41] when someone falls through stumbling (*'skandal-
izetai'*).
   The picture of the Apostle, who amid his own trials is still consumed by care for his Churches, is most moving. We also see that, during

[37] The word *'pseudadelphos'* is found again in Galatians 2³. It is not found elsewhere in the Bible or in secular writing; it is probably therefore a coining of Paul.
[38] Another explanation, which we believe to be ill-founded, has been put forward by J. MÜLLER-BARDORFF, cf. *supra* our note on 6⁵.
[39] Windisch remarks here that iconography has, generally speaking, depicted
Paul as too well dressed and too well fed. But we know that historical truth was in
general the last thing to bother Christian artists.
[40] Allo translates as 'tension' however. W. Bauer: 'strained attention.' Windisch, for his part, refers to Acts 24¹² and to 2 Maccabees 6³.
[41] Osty translates *'puroumai'* as 'a fire consumes me,' which comes to almost
the same thing. Crampon: 'I am on fire.'

his journeys, and no doubt especially during his stays in towns, Paul found ways of receiving letters or messengers to keep him informed, a point which is confirmed by many passages in his letters.[42]

11[30] now gives the precise sense of '*kauchasthai*' in **11[18]**; as far back as the Old Testament it is written that a man should *boast* only of divine help. For the Apostle this help is all the more effective because he confesses his own weakness (cf. below **12[5,9]**).[43]

11[31], using a brief doxology, calls on God as witness to his truthfulness; what is involved then is a kind of oath (cf. **1[23]**; **11[10]**).

11[32–33] add as a coda a fresh episode, dramatic if not tragic: the flight from Damascus.[44] As is well known, the event also appears in Acts 9[24]. But the two accounts differ in one curious detail. Whilst according to Acts the danger came from the Jews, here it is the governor of the Arabian king Aretas who bears the grudge. Obviously the present text, as first-hand information, should have preference. The version in Acts is, however, not necessarily without value, since the Jews may have intrigued with the authorities against Paul.[45]

Who was this Aretas? We know of several Arabian 'kings' of this name.[46] The only one to take into account here is Aretas IV, head of the Nabataean kingdom (to the east of Palestine), who reigned from 9 B.C. to about A.D. 39. It is thought that in A.D. 34 he recaptured Damascus,[47] a town which had already been taken by one of his predecessors, but which had fallen into Roman hands in 63 B.C. So Paul's flight could be placed between A.D. 34 and 39. If the visit to Damascus in question is that following his conversion, a date as close as possible to A.D. 34 must obviously be chosen. Yet Galatians 1[17] mentions a second visit to Damascus, separated from the first by a stay in 'Arabia' of unspecified duration. It is also to be noted that even if Aretas controlled only the surrounding countryside and not the

---

[42] See for example 1 Corinthians 1[11]; 5[1]; 7[1]; 16[7]; as well as the journeys of Titus and Timothy.

[43] Cf. R. BULTMANN, '*kauchaomai*', etc., *TWNT*, III, pp. 646ff.

[44] GOUDGE, *Westminster Commentary*, p. 110, also BALJON *De Tekst der brieven van Paulus an de Romeinen, de Corinthiers*, etc., Utrecht 1884, p. 159, and others, would like to erase these verses as a gloss, since the recital of the 'peristases' seems to be completed. But the Apostle may well have asked Timothy to add this remark afterwards; *sic* Windisch.—P. COUCHOUD, *RHR*, 1923, p. 12, places vv. 32–3 after v. 25, where their appearance would be even more bizarre.

[45] That the writer of the Acts should have overstated the rôle of the Jews would be in keeping with his leading idea of the systematic rejection of Paulinism by the Jews of the diaspora.

[46] On the chief ones, cf. PAULY–WISSOWA, *sub*. Aretas.

[47] But the only evidence is supplied by the absence of Roman coinage after A.D. 34.

city itself, he could have mounted a guard over 'the gates of the city' (Acts 9²⁴) from outside in order to seize Paul as he left the city. In any event the Apostle was constrained to make a clandestine departure.

Details: *'Thuris'* means a 'window'. As it is stated that the Apostle passed 'through the wall' (*'dia tou teichous'*), it can only mean a window set in the wall which at the same time formed the exterior wall of a house.[48] He was let down in a basket (*'en sarganē'*).[49]

---

[48] In any case *'dia tou teichous'* must not be translated as 'over the wall' or 'along the wall.' This interpretation is philologically impossible as well as being a contradiction of the mention of a window.—An example of a house built up to the wall of a town and equipped with a window is moreover given by the house of Rahab in Jericho (Josh 2¹⁵⁻¹⁸).

[49] In itself this stratagem has nothing humiliating about it. Some eastern monasteries, like the convent of St Catherine at Sinai, normally welcome visitors by hoisting them up in a basket.

CHAPTER XII

(1) *I am obliged to boast, even though it does no good. So I will come to visions and revelations of the Lord. (2) I know a Christian who fourteen years ago—was it in the body? I do not know; was it out of the body? I do not know, God knows—this man was borne away to the third heaven. (3) And I know that this man—was it in the body or out of the body? I do not know, God knows—(4) was borne away to paradise and heard ineffable words which it is not permitted to repeat. (5) It is of this man that I shall avail myself; but I shall not avail myself of my own case, unless it be about my weaknesses. (6) For if I shall wish to boast, I shall not be mad; for I shall speak the truth. But I speak of myself with some reserve, for fear of arousing an impression of myself superior to that suggested by my appearance and speech. (7) And so that the abundance of revelations should not puff me up, a thorn has been thrust into my flesh: an angel of Satan with orders to harass me. (8) Three times I prayed the Lord about it, that it should leave me. (9) But He told me 'my grace is sufficient for you; for my strength is displayed in weakness.' Therefore I would much rather boast of my weaknesses, so that the power of Christ should rest on me. (10) That is why I delight in my misfortunes: insults, distresses, persecutions, sufferings endured for Christ. For when I am weak, then I am strong.*

12¹⁻¹⁰ Here a 'foolish discourse' of a new kind begins (with the oratorical caveat 'although it is not good, that is to say profitable'). There is nothing more about hardships and weaknesses, at least in the early part, but of certain exceptional graces granted to an '*anthrōpos en Christō*,' that is to a Christian.[1] It is a matter of 'visions' ('*optasiai*') and 'revelations' ('*apokalupseis*'). The genitive '*tou kuriou*' may mean appearances of the Lord or visions given by the Lord. The carrying away to the third heaven (v. 2) could point towards the second interpretation. For the appearances of the Lord on the Damascus road or in the Temple at Jerusalem involve no necessity for being 'carried away.' The translation to paradise (v. 4) seems to be the same as to the third heaven; at least according to Slavonic Enoch it is in the third heaven that paradise is to be found.[2]

---

[1] The use of the third person is to avoid an over-egocentric expression. In Aramaic also '*bar nash*' or '*bar nasha*' is often used for the first person. The Gospel writers translate such expressions by '*huios tou anthrōpou*.' Cf. for example Mark 8³¹ or Matthew 8²⁰; but it goes without saying that in the Gospels, the word has another sense also. See our *Royaume de Dieu*, 1938, pp. 88–110.

[2] Cf. Slavonic Enoch, the long recension, Ch. 8, trans. Vaillant (cf. Bibliography).

12²⁻⁴ make up a stanza of two parallel members, in the Hebrew style. For understanding the translation Windisch (p. 369) refers to the Philonic distinction between the 'self' which leaves the body and the man as such. But with Paul it is the man as such ('*anthrōpos*') who is carried away! It must also be noted that the Apostle remembers the revelations, a detail which does not favour the theory of a split between two personalities. All that can be said is that his person may have left the body. Yet even Paul is not sure of this. For he states that he was ignorant of whether he was transported with or without body. That he should have envisaged the first possibility may seem strange. But the Jews were acquainted with the bodily return journeys of Enoch into the supernatural realms,[3] as well as with the final bodily removal of Enoch and Elijah.

12³ Concerning the third heaven, it is worth recalling, once again, that belief in the plurality of the heavens is attested by the constant use of the plural '*šamayim*' = 'the heavens' (in Greek, '*ouranoi*'[4]). But how many heavens did the Rabbis and apocalyptic writers know? Generally speaking, seven are mentioned.[5] If it is supposed—the view we adopt—that vv. 2 and 3 tell of the same event, then they evidently place 'paradise' in the third heaven. This, in effect, is the ouranology of the Apocalypse of Moses[6] and of Slavonic Enoch.[7]

Could this paradise be that of Genesis, subsequently borne away to heaven, or else its celestial counterpart? It is difficult to be definite on this point.[8] According to Revelation 2[7] only at the end of time will

---

[3] According to Ethiopic Enoch 12[1] the pre-Flood patriarch disappeared with his body, to reappear in Ch. 81[5].

[4] See *The Vocabulary of the Bible*, art. 'Heaven'.

[5] Testament of Levi 3[1]; Slavonic Enoch, Chs 8–22 in the B redaction; Ascension of Isaiah, Ch. 9.—However in the A redaction of the same Enoch there are ten, and the Greek Apocalypse of Baruch Chs 1–11 speaks of five heavens. But the Talmud and Midrash stick to the notion of seven heavens. Cf. Talm.Bab. Chagiga 11b, which gives the names of the seven heavens, as do other texts quoted in *TWNT* V, p. 511, n. 96; see also the classic work of W. BACHER, *Die Aggada der Tannaiten* II, p. 56 and n. 3 (Strasburg 1890).

As for the monograph of ILDEFONSE DE VUIPPENS, *Le paradis terrestre au troisième ciel*, Paris and Friburg in Switz. 1925, its value resides especially in the information about the different heavens of the Greeks, among whom the seven heavens corresponded to the seven planets. Contrarily to the Hebrews, they counted downwards, the highest heaven being called the first.

[6] Cf. 40[2], 'away to Paradise in the third heaven' (CHARLES, II, p. 151).

[7] 8[1] (Vaillant's trans. 5[1]) 'and the two men . . . took me to the third heaven and placed me in the midst of paradise' (B redaction only).

[8] Others placed paradise on earth at the end of the world. It is obviously not Paul's conception. It is known that '*paradeisos*' (Persian root) means 'park' or 'garden' (cf. XENOPHON, *Anabasis*, I, 2, the '*paradeisos megas agriōn thēriōn plērēs*', park full of large wild animals, belonging to Cyrus). It is not surprising then that the LXX translated (in Gen 2[8]) '*gan* b[e] '*eden*' (garden of Eden) by '*paradeisos en Edem*.' In the N.T. paradise is mentioned only in Luke 23[43] and Revelation 2[7]. Cf. *TWNT* V, pp. 763ff.

the elect enjoy paradise. Paul therefore received the extraordinary privilege of being able to enter in advance.[9]

12[4] The expression *'arrhēta rhēmata'* = 'ineffable words' may be borrowed from the language of the mystery religions, in which initiates in a supranormal state could hear words uttered by the gods, about which it was necessary either to observe complete silence or pass on information only to the elect and under the pledge of secrecy.[10] It can be seen that *'arrhētos'* does not necessarily mean 'inexpressible in human language,' but at all events *forbidden to divulge*. The same applies in **12[4]** where *'ouk exon lalēsai'* can only mean: *it is forbidden* for a man *to utter them*.[11] It is useless then to seek the content of those revelations in the Apostle's letters!

We learn nothing precise about the circumstances of the event. One clue only about the date is given—fourteen years ago, **12[2]**—which is enough to eliminate any connection with the vision on the Damascus road, which moreover is phenomenologically presented very differently.[12] Indeed if our Epistle was written *circa* A.D. 56, the event must be placed in about A.D. 42, that is at a period much later than the first stay in Damascus and of which we know nothing except that the Apostle was in Syria and Cilicia (Gal 1[21]).[13]

12[5] may again give the impression that the Apostle distinguishes two personalities within himself: the man (*'anthrōpos'*) who received special outpourings of grace, and himself (*'emautou'*), who has no reason to boast. However, there seems to be no question of a real duality, but merely of a distinction between two aspects of his being. Moreover the terminology is quite different from that of the mystics who speak of the 'self' being borne away to higher worlds, as we have already insisted.

---

[9] Does Jewish literature have records of any men, Enoch apart, who entered paradise? Apparently there were four, all Rabbis. The first died as a result, the second fell ill, the third was severely beaten by an angel; only R. Aqiba returned 'in peace,' Talm.Bab.Chagiga, 14b–15b.—As for the 'good robber' of Luke 23[43], obviously he would attain it only at his death.—Note also that according to Revelation 2[7] the Tree of Life is still to be found in paradise.

[10] Many references in WINDISCH, pp. 377ff. An interesting thing is that Philo also knew this language. See for example *Quod deterius potiori insidiari soleat* (That the worse is wont to attack the better) Chapter 48 § 175 where he explains that it is fortunate for the untutored to be 'dull-witted' and 'deaf', otherwise it would be necessary to cut out their tongues to 'save them from uttering anything that should not be divulged' (*'huper tou mēden tōn arrhētōn eklalēsai'*).

[11] So Paul remembered what was revealed to him. Only the circumstances of his translation (in the body or not) have been forgotten.

[12] On the Damascus road there was no taking-up, but an opening of the heavens (*'ek tou ouranou'*, Acts 22[6]; *'ouranothen'*, 26[13]*).

[13] In Acts 22[17] Paul mentions an 'ecstasy' in the Temple. But he reports the words which he heard.

S.E.C.—8

12⁶ points to a further motive for the writer's reserve about his revelations: he does not wish to be overestimated; this is why he boasts only of his weakness. He should be judged only on what can be seen and heard and not on unascertainable occurrences. *'Pheidomai'* = 'I treat kindly' the recipients, I do not wish to crush them; *'eis eme logizesthai'* = 'to reckon to my account'; nothing should be reckoned to his account but what is self-evident.

12⁷ *'Tē huperbolē tōn apokalupseōn'* could in principle allude to a great number of 'revelations'; but it is the sense of 'outstanding quality' which alone is suitable for *'huperbolē'* here; the question of quantity does not arise. We also think that this group of words should be taken with what follows, and that *'dio'* should be dropped as occurs in many excellent witnesses,[14] as well as the full-stop inserted by Nestlé before this conjunction. The sense of **12⁷** is then quite clear: in order that the Apostle should not set himself above what is fitting (*'hine mē huperairōmai'*) as a consequence of his revelations, a thorn or affliction (*'skolops'*) in the flesh has been given him, and it is defined as a messenger of Satan, who must 'harass' him.[15] It goes without saying that neither Satan nor his 'angel' acted without divine authorisation. But what is the malady or other torment of which the writer speaks? Many hypotheses have been advanced, the list of which can be found in the recent studies by Ph. Menoud and H. Clavier.[16]

Menoud sees the thorn and the blows as the Apostle's persistent anguish about the destiny of the Jewish people, who as a whole reject the gospel and seem to make a lie of the divine promises to the nation.[17]

[14] Nestlé lists p 46, D, all the Latin and Syriac versions, Origen, Irenaeus. Once more the so-called Western text which was read everywhere by everyone in the second century shows up as the most intelligent. As for the so-called Caesarean text (3rd century) on which *grosso modo* p 45 and p 46 draw, we consider this to be the 'Western' text on its way to becoming the Alexandrine text (4th century).

[15] It is possible that *'anggelos'* has its technical sense here. In that case it concerns an angel who has fallen into the devil's service. But the malady, sent by Satan, may also have been personified.—The repetition of *'hina mē huperairōmai'* at the end of the verse is superfluous and should be erased as is done in S, A, D and the Latin versions.

[16] H. CLAVIER, 'La santé de l'apôtre Paul'; PH. MENOUD, 'L'écharde et l'ange satanique'. Both articles are in *Studia Paulina in honorem Johannes de Zwaan septuagenario* (Haarlem 1953), pp. 66ff and 163ff respectively.—For *'skolops'* cf. also Ezekiel 28²⁴, where this term is taken in the moral sense.

[17] It must be recognised that this anguish was real. Several solutions of this serious problem will be given in the Epistle to the Romans. At times the Apostle sees in 'Israel according to the Spirit,' that is in Christians, the true inheritors of the promises, at others in a 'remnant', and at others—his definitive position seemingly—he hopes for the conversion of Israel 'in the end.'

Other interpreters agree in viewing it as a physical handicap suggested by '*tē sarki*'.[18] What handicap? A fairly widely held hypothesis sees it as an eye complaint.[19]

A further quite widespread theory is epilepsy. There is no textual support for such an affliction. True, we are referred to the event on the Damascus road, where the Apostle collapsed. But why should the vision not be the *cause* of the collapse, as texts elsewhere suggest (Acts 9^3; 22^6; 26^{13-14})? We pass over the other suggested ailments— neuralgia (Tertullian), colic, malaria, severe attacks of rheumatism, leprosy, etc.—in order to mention the more original opinion of Clavier, who, taking account of the context, diagnoses a disorder of the nervous system, caused by terrible hardships as well as by spiritual shocks due to visions and revelations.

In view of the difficulty of reaching a satisfactory conclusion, the reader will forgive us for ending with a *non liquet*. But it seems certain that the 'blows' ('*kolaphizō*)' of the 'angel' were a serious handicap for the Apostle's missionary work. This is the main reason why Paul (**12⁸**) three times asked the Lord ('*kurios*'),[20] that is Christ, to deliver him from them. These three prayers recall the three requests of Jesus in Gethsemane, but also, in a more general way, the importance attributed by the Jews to the number three in invocations as well as in blessings.[21]

The answer was negative (**12⁹**), but accompanied by an assurance: 'my grace is sufficient,' namely to continue the task. The perfect '*eirēken*' = 'he said' seems to indicate clearly the definite nature of the answer. The end of v. 9 also forms part of the answer, a part which St Paul took so much to heart that 'strength being fulfilled in weakness' became one of his great certitudes. '*Dunamis Christou*' = 'the power of Christ' is almost personified here. It rests on Paul (for '*episkēnoō*' = lit. 'to pitch one's tent somewhere,' cf. Jn 1^{14}). The

---

[18] We know, however, that '*sarx*' can also be the earthly human level on which relationships between members of a natural family operate. See 1 Corinthians 7^{28}. '*Tē sarki*' could then, in principle, also refer to the Jewish people of which Paul is a part, cf. the expression 'Israel according to the flesh' ('*kata sarka*') and *similia* 1 Corinthians 10^{18}; Romans 1^3; 9^3.

[19] Galatians 6^{11} is cited ('See with what large letters I am writing to you') and Galatians 4^{15} ('If possible, you would have plucked out your eyes—to give them to me'). Neither of these texts is conclusive.

[20] This text is undeniably the only Pauline passage which expressly attests a prayer addressed to Christ and not to God the Father. But the expression '*hoi epikaloumenoi to onoma tou kuriou hēmōn Iesou Christou*' shows that his invocation was not unusual (see, for example, Acts 9^{14}).

[21] According to Midrash Tehouma 22.2 (quoted as in WINDISCH, p. 389), Esther's prayer was answered after she had prayed three times. According to Psalm 55^{18} (54^{18}) one should pray three times a day. Cf. STADE, 'Die Dreizahl im A.T.', *ZAW*, 1906, p. 124.

(11) *I have just been playing the fool. You made me do it. For my defence should have been your responsibility. Indeed, I have been in no way inferior to the 'transcendent apostles,' even though I do not count.* (12) *The distinctive signs of an apostle were accomplished among you with perfect constancy: miracles, wonders and [other] deeds of power.* (13) *What did you have to envy in other Churches, if it were not that I for my part did not live at your expense? Forgive me this wrong!*

Jews had long spoken of the glory of God (Shekinah or Kabod) resting on the elect.[22]

12[10] '*Eudokeō*'[23] = 'I delight in' evidently contains a grandiose paradox, almost even more curious than the idea of glorification. '*Hubris*' in the plural signifies not only attitudes but especially *insolent actions*.[24]

'*Anangkē*' is etymologically and semantically the equivalent of 'anguish'; '*diōgmos*' = 'persecution'; '*stenochōria*' = 'a narrow space,' 'impasse' (almost synonymous with '*anangkē*').

12[10b] 'When . . .' sums up the idea of vv. 9 and 10a in a magnificent aphorism. It loses nothing of its grandeur, if we note that Philo sometimes expresses himself similarly.[25]

12[11-13] In 12[11] the author once again asserts that he would not have 'played the fool' if some of his recipients had duly upheld him or spoken up for him ('*sunistasthai*'); '*huperlian*' see *ad loc.* 11[5]—'*ei kai ouden eimi*' = 'even if I am nothing' (hypothetical) or 'although . . .' (concessive). We translate as 'even though,' which has a little of both senses (same remark for 11[6]).[26] The expression 'I am nothing' is

---

[22] According to Talmud Bab.Nedarim 38a (GOLDSCHMIDT V, p. 443), R. Johannan said 'The Holy One, blessed be He, causes His divinity to rest on him who is strong and rich and wise and humble.' This text is given as a commentary on the appearances of God (in the cloud) to Moses, according to Exodus 19[9] or Numbers 12[2-5]. Yet these passages speak only of the cloud as placing itself *before* the man of God. But it is possible that the expression '*episkēnoō*' in the Apostle's writing was suggested by the tent ('*skēnē*') at the entrance of which the cloud took up its position according to Numbers 12[5].

[23] '*Eudokeō*' could at a pinch mean 'I am satisfied.'

[24] A '*hubristēs*' is a brawler. The '*hubristika*' at Argos were feasts which allowed the women to behave haughtily.

[25] *Vita Mosis* I, § 67 and 69, p. 91, '*to asthenes hēmōn dunamis estin*' (our weakness is might). In this passage the Rabbi of Alexandria speculates about the burning bush (Ex 3) in which he sees a symbol of the righteous man who finds strength in misfortune, instead of being consumed by it. But it is not clear whether the wise man draws his strength from God or from his own Stoic virtue, a solution which is absolutely ruled out in Paul.—Still less did the Apostle think of boasting of an automatic moral education through misfortune. He knew only too well that adversity carries the risk of making faithless men worse.

[26] Allo, Goguel, Osty choose the concessive sense.

(14) *Here I am ready to come among you for the third time;
and I shall not be a charge upon you; for it is not your goods that I
seek, but yourselves. Indeed, it is not the duty of children to economise
for their parents, but of parents for their children.* (15) *As for myself,
I will gladly incur expenses and will spend myself to the utmost for
your souls. Must it be, because I love you too much, that I should be
less loved?*

without doubt not invented by Paul;[27] but he uses it to sum up in
something of a hyperbole the Corinthians' uncomplimentary judgement of his person.

12^{12} lists proofs of his apostleship (as Rom 15^{19}), for the benefit of
others be it understood (for himself, he found the proof in his apostolic vocation). '*Sēmeion*' = 'sign'; at first this word has a fairly
broad sense, but in v. 12 it is synonymous with 'miracle', or even with
a certain kind of miracle, if a distinction is sought between '*sēmeia*',
'*terata*' = 'wonders' and '*dunameis*' = 'acts of power.' But it is
possible that '*sēmeia kai terata*' was already a current phrase (a kind
of hendiadys),[28] and that '*dunameis*' was then reserved for healings,
as in the Gospels. But the threefold formula is also found in the New
Testament,[29] so that there should perhaps be not too much insistence
on any distinction between the three terms. In any case, in addition to
healings, such things as exorcisms, excommunications, foretelling the
future, glossolalia, thought-reading (cf. 1 Cor 12) must have been
involved, but not appearances which were unascertainable by third
parties. '*En pasē hupomonē*' might lead us to think of including the
Apostle's perseverance among the proofs (*sic* Allo, Osty); but is it a
proof of apostleship? And would the expression not be rather pale as
a summary of the near-superhuman courage of the Apostle in his
besetting difficulties? We prefer (with B.d.Cent.) to render it 'with
perfect constancy' (or regularity) in the performance of signs, etc.

12^{13-15} The Corinthians seem to have been jealous of the other
Churches. But Paul denies that they had the slightest reason to doubt

---

[27] See EPICTETUS, *Discourses*, III, 9.14: '*ouden ēn Epiktētos*' ('Epictetus was
nothing at all'); cf. IV, 8.25: '*ei ge tis blapsai dunatai, egō ouden poiō · ei allon
perimenō, hina me ōpheilēsē, ouden eimi*' ('if a man can hurt me, what I am engaged
in amounts to nothing; if I wait for somebody else to help me, I am myself nothing').
[28] In John 4^{48}, Mark 13^{22} and many passages in Acts, as well as in the LXX
and Josephus (cf. PREUSCHEN–BAUER, *sub.* '*sēmeion*'). It must be noted, moreover,
that in the well-known passage 1 Corinthians 12^{28} on charisms, the gift of miracles
is not listed as specifically apostolic. If the Apostle insists on this charism here (in
principle unessential for him), it is in order not to trail behind the Jerusalem
Apostles, who ascribed a primordial importance to it; cf. especially Matthew 10^8;
Luke 10^{19}; Acts 2^{43}; 3^{6-8}; 4^{30}; 5^5.
[29] Acts 2^{22}.

(16) *Agreed [someone will say], I personally have not been a burden to you. But as I am capable of anything, I took you by trickery!* (17) *Take any one of those whom I sent to you: is it claimed that I exploited you through him?* (18) *[Thus] I asked Titus [to come to you] and with him I sent the brother. Is it claimed that Titus exploited you, in however small a way? Did we not make our way in the same spirit? tread the same tracks?*

his affection. There is in truth only one point on which they were 'at a disadvantage' (again sarcastic language!): the Apostle has committed the 'injustice' of never living at their expense (cf. 1 Cor 9), and he will continue to observe this rule (v. 14).—'*Autos egō*' (not quite the same emphasis as in **10¹**) = 'I alone' in contrast with the false apostles. He has not sought after their goods, but themselves, that is their good. '*Psuchē*' = 'life', true life being understood.—Like good parents, who economise ('*thēsaurizein*') for their children, he will spend utterly the little which he possesses and he will also spend himself ('*dapanēsō kai ekdapanthēsomai*'), again a happy and terse turn of phrase to show his lack of self-seeking. But let us return to **12¹⁴ᵃ**. He announces a third visit, the first being evidently the one narrated in Acts 18 (founding of the Church), the second the one announced in 1 Corinthians 16 and occurring before the writing of **10–13**.³⁰

12¹⁶⁻¹⁸ Thoroughly distressed by the attacks of his adversaries, the Apostle brings forward one of their arguments, heard or guessed at. Indeed, Paul may have asked his congregation for nothing, but this was in order to take them by imposture ('*panourgos*') or by deceit ('*dolō*').³¹ What is the significance of this accusation? From what follows in v. 17 we may suppose that the calumny was aimed at the visit of an associate, Titus for example, whom Paul could use as an intermediary in an attempt to exploit the Corinthians ('*di' autou epleonektēsa*').³² The Apostle vigorously defends his helper against

³⁰ We attach '*triton touto*' to '*elthein*' and not to '*hetoimōs*' (third preparation for travelling, the second not having been followed by the deed). For as ALLO points out, p. 326, the statement in **13¹** requires the first interpretation.
Expositors who do not admit a visit between 1 and 2 Corinthians are obliged to accept the interpretation which we have just rejected, for instance N. D. J. WHITE, 'The visits of S. Paul to Corinth,' Review *Hermathena*, vol. 28, 1903, V, 78f.

³¹ '*Panourgos*' is a *hapax legomenon* in the N.T., but it is found in the LXX. The word means a man 'capable of anything' ('*pan-ergon*'). Liddell–Scott render it very well 'ready to do anything.' To translate this insult by 'crafty' weakens its impact. Similarly '*dolos*' often has, and here without a shadow of doubt, a stronger sense than 'cunning' (deceit or lack of integrity).

³² The construction in v.17, in which the accusative '*tina*' is picked up by '*di' autou*,' can be found in common speech and in modern Greek, see BLASS–DE-BRUNNER § 466.1.—In v. 18, Windisch supposes that '*hina erchētai pros humas*' (or the like) should be added after '*parekalesa*'. This does not mean that the phrase was actually written and disappeared later.

(19) *Once more, you must be thinking that we are justifying ourselves to you. Now it is beneath the gaze of God that we speak as Christians. But all this, my dear friends, is done for your edification.* (20) *For I am very afraid that at my coming I shall not find you as I should wish, and you similarly will find me as you would not wish. I dread to find among you discord, fanaticism, animosity, quarrels, calumny, gossip, conceit, disorder.* (21) *Grant that at my coming visit God should not humiliate me before you and that I do not have to be chief mourner over many former sinners unreturned from [the life] of impurity, fornication and debauchery which they had led.*

such insinuations. In fact he works in the same spirit as himself ('*tō autō pneumati*'). He follows the same paths.

Once more, we note the anonymity of Titus' companion, who is merely referred to as '*adelphos*' (cf. 8[18]). As for Titus' mission, it must refer to a visit prior to the one announced in **8** and **9**, if, as we think, **10**–**13** are of earlier date than the other chapters.

12[19] '*Palai*' = 'for a long time,' adopted by Nestlé, is strange. Certain witnesses[33] read '*palin*' = 'again', a reading which gives better sense. For the Corinthians might think ('*dokeite*') that Paul wishes, once more ('*palin*'), to give his apologia ('*apologoumetha*'). But is this not correct? No, if by 'apologia' we understand, as the author seems to do here, a *biassed* defence. He declares before God that it is nothing of the kind; for he speaks 'in Christ,' that is as a selfless Christian, whose only aim is edification, though without concealment of his anxieties.

12[20–21] gives, in fact, a list of vices which seem to prevail in Corinth, a list which recalls the one in Galatians 5[20] and to some extent the one in Romans 1[29]ff. The wording presents almost no difficulties (see our translation) except that the clearly bad sense taken by '*zēlos*' = 'fanaticism'[34] must be noted. In the face of this spirit of squabble and intrigue, the Apostle is afraid that he will be obliged to punish (cf. **10**[2]), to sadden ('*penthēsai*') many unrepentant sinners ('*proēmartē-kotōn kai mē metanoēsantōn*'). As he adds to the list of sins impurity ('*akatharsia*'), fornication ('*porneia*') and lewd behaviour ('*aselgeia*'), one would like to think that the pagan past of some of the Corinthians

---

[33] The Textus Receptus, D and the Syriac.—P 46 reads '*ou palai*' which is probably an emendation.
[34] In contrast with 11[2]; 7[7]; 9[2]; Romans 10[2]; Philippians 3[6]; Colossians 4[13].—The bad sense (jealousy, fanaticism, severity) is also found in 1 Corinthians 3[3]; 7[11]; Romans 13[13]; Galatians 5[20], cf. '*zēloō*' 1 Corinthians 13[4].—'*Psithurismos*' (Windisch: 'whispering', 'tale-bearing') indicates calumnies whispered in a neighbour's ear; cf. the well-known 'whispering campaign' or 'quiet propaganda' so feared by certain governments. The original sense of '*psithurizō*' seems to be 'to twitter.'

is in question (cf. Rom 1²⁶ᶠᶠ); but passages like 1 Corinthians 5; 8¹²⁻²⁰ show that serious excesses sometimes still occurred among Church members.³⁵ On the other hand, our text shows that the Apostle believes in the possibility of repentance and readmission into the Church of 'grave' sinners.³⁶

But why does the Apostle fear (cf. beginning of v. 21) that God wishes to humiliate him ('*tapeinōsē*') once more ('*palin*') before the Corinthians? It seems to carry an allusion to the preceding visit, also mentioned in 10¹ ('*tapeinos*'). But since the Apostle has decided to show himself forceful, the feared humiliation must be a purely moral one, because he will have to be ashamed of his congregation before God (cf. 7¹⁴; 9⁴).

---

³⁵ Sometimes '*porneia*' has a technical sense: immorality in connection with the cult of Aphrodite, which was very flourishing in Corinth. Cf. the Baal cults among the Canaanites.

³⁶ The Epistle to the Hebrews seems to teach the opposite (6⁴⁻⁸). But on close examination, that writing deals only with a particular type of apostasy. See our Commentary *L'épître aux Hébreux*. (ET in preparation.)

CHAPTER XIII

(1) *This is the third visit that I shall pay to you. 'Every matter will be decided on the word of two or three witnesses.'* (2) *At the time of my second visit (and I repeat it now that I am absent), I had already declared to former sinners and to all the others: if I return, I shall not spare you.* (3) *You want proof, do you not, that Christ speaks through me, and He does not show Himself weak in your eyes, but manifests His power among you?* (4) *Certainly He was crucified on account of His*

13¹ᵃ Cf. our interpretation of **12¹⁴**.

13¹ᵇ is a quotation from the law of Deuteronomy 19¹⁵, also quoted in Matthew 18¹⁶, there too on a point of ecclesiastical discipline. But why does the Apostle have an interest in underlining that two or three witnesses will be necessary? Is it merely to give the enquiry a character of absolute correctness (*sic* Schlatter, p. 433)? Or are the three visits the equivalent of three witnesses?[1] At first sight this assimilation may seem strange, but the Apostle may have interpreted this commandment in a fairly broad, almost allegorical sense, in the manner of the Rabbis.

13² *'Proeirēka'* = 'I have already said previously' refers to the second visit (*'parōn to deuteron'*), and *'prolegō'* = 'I say in advance,' to the letter which he is writing while absent (*'apōn nun'*).[2]

What is the content of this 'prediction'? The announcement of his severity towards those who were mentioned in **12²¹**, namely, the old unrepentant sinners, as well as 'all the others,' because they had not reacted seriously.—*'Ou pheisomai'* = 'I shall not restrain myself,' or 'I shall show no tenderness' (B.d.Cent.: 'I shall be pitiless').

13³ implies that the Corinthians fancied themselves stronger than the Apostle and thought that he would never have the courage to show proof (*'dokimē'*) of apostolic authority; that is why he recalls that Christ speaks in him, and Christ will show His power (*'ouk asthenei alla dunatei'*).

---

[1] *Sic* CHRYSOSTOM (*MPG* 61, col. 590), Calvin, and a great number of modern exegetes, e.g. Plummer, Bachmann, Windisch. Against: Allo.—THEODORET simply said *'anti tōn prosōpōn ta pragmata tetheiken'* (he laid the matters before them).

[2] The Textus Receptus and the Syriac versions add *'graphō'*, which would duplicate *'prolegō'*.

*weakness, but He is alive through the power of God. Similarly with us:
we are weak in Him, but we shall be alive with Him through the power of
God, in your presence. (5) Put yourselves to the test, if [as you claim]
you are indeed in the faith; make yourselves take this examination. Or
do you not recognise that Jesus Christ is in you? (Unless the proof
turns against you.) (6) But you will understand, I hope, that we [also]
shall endure the test. (7) However, we pray God that we may not have*

13⁴ It is true that Christ was crucified 'in weakness' ('*ex astheneias*');
but He lives through the power of God ('*ek dunameōs theou*'). The
Apostle shares in His weakness (cf. **11** and **12**), but also in His
strength.[3] In any case death and resurrection with Christ is one of
the fundamental themes of what is called by general consent 'Pauline
mysticism.' For the Apostle the death and resurrection are not only
historical events which caused a cosmic upheaval by the victory over
the devil and the 'powers', but become constituent elements in the
personal life of Christians, something which the Apostle experienced
in a particularly dramatic way.[4]

13⁵ urges the readers to make what we call today an examination of
their conscience, or, in certain cases, a 'self-criticism'. Let them ex-
amine themselves, therefore ('*peirazete heautous*'); let them test
themselves[5] ('*heautous dokimazete*'), in order to see whether they are
'in the faith,'[6] that is to say anchored in the new existence which is

[3] We may wonder why the Apostle uses here the future ('*zēsomen*' or '*zēsometha*'
according to some witnesses); perhaps this formula was suggested to him by the
one he used concerning the resurrection (cf. Rom 6⁴). This would mean a slight
slip of the pen by the author or by Timothy.—But it may also be claimed that he
is thinking of his appearance in Corinth, which is in the future. Then the words
'*eis humas*,' missing in B and D³, must be retained. Even so the plural is curious.
P 46 reads '*zōn*' instead of '*zēsomen*', a reading of little interest. (Some witnesses,
notably the Vulgate, Syriac and Marcion, read '*ei*' before '*estaurōthē*', but this is
harmless.)

[4] It goes without saying that this 'resurrection' in Christ comprises two aspects,
or, if it is preferred, two stages; the new life on earth, made possible by the
possession of the Holy Spirit, and the bodily resurrection (or transformation)
which represents the eschatological side. The two stages are closely linked
through the formation of an 'inner man' in believers, which is the germ of the
resurrection man, which will be made manifest (Rom 8¹⁹) at the parousia.

[5] In the language of the late period the third person reflexive pronoun ('*heautous*', etc.) is also used for the second and even for the first person. This fact is so
well known that we do not labour it.

[6] There has been much discussion in order to ascertain whether '*pistis*' in
Paul's work means rather an attitude of man (trust) or a virtue of God (faithfulness); see K. BARTH, *Epistle to the Romans*. We think that both senses are
found. But there is a third, a very important one, in which '*pistis*' conjures up a
new *situation*, that of normal relationships with God, with all which that situation implies.

reason to treat you roughly; for our preoccupation is not to give mani-
fest proof [of our authority], but to see you doing good, even if we must
appear as not having given our proofs. (8) For we can do nothing against
the truth, but [only] for the truth. (9) And so we rejoice when we are

that of the Christian, and which implies the presence of Christ 'in
us.'[7] It is hoped that the Corinthians will not be ploughed (*'adokimoi'*)
in the test.

13[6] But it is also hoped that the recipients will recognise that the
Apostle and his helpers are not *'adokimoi'*, that they will be 'able to
endure the test.'[8] This way of appealing to the Christian conscience
of his flock instead of crushing them with his apostolic authority,
bears witness to a comprehensive pedagogical approach, comparable
to that of the Gospel, which seeks to awaken mankind.

13[7] is not difficult, if *'humas'* is taken as the subject of *'poiēsai'*. The
Apostle is then praying to God (*'euchometha'*) that the Corinthians
do no more evil. This fits well with what follows: *'hina humeis to
kalon poiēte'* = 'in order that you may do good.' According to
another interpretation, *'humas'* (at the beginning of the verse) is the
object of *'poiēsai'*, the subject of which is the Apostle; in this case the
Apostle wishes not to be obliged to do evil to the Corinthians, that is
by punishing them. We have preferred the first explanation, to which
we are led by the words *'ouch hina hēmeis . . .'* = 'not in order to
appear justified' (*'dokimoi'*), namely in your eyes, as well as by the
reason already indicated. The choice of the good life will indeed be a
way of proving the Apostle right. But that will not be the motive of
the prayer: he will be ready to accept defeat (*'hēmeis hōs adokimoi
ōmen'*), provided they do good. Care about the salvation of the
members takes precedence even over his authority among them.

13[8] This verse's maxim, which has a quite general application, was
undoubtedly not framed *ad hoc*. *'Alētheia'* = 'truth', but also 'righteousness'.[9] The Apostle is not free to act against it because it is
fixed by God. But why did he insert the phrase here? Primarily to

---

[7] For the study of this theme, we refer readers to Albert Schweitzer (see Bibliography), but without accepting his thesis which sees in Pauline mysticism first and
foremost an effort of *thought*, which is more or less 'Gnostic'.—Consult also A.
WIKENHAUSER, *Die Christusmystik des Apostels Paulus*, 2nd edn, Friburg in
Brisgau 1956, and the discussion of the question by J. B. ČOLON, 'A propos de la
mystique de saint Paul,' *Revue des Sciences religieuses*, XV, 1935, pp. 157–83
and 325–53.

[8] There is, however, a nuance in the manner in which *'adokimos'* is used in v. 6
and v. 7 respectively. In the Apostle's case, there is no question of an examination
of conscience, but of proof of his capacities, there is therefore almost a play on
words.

[9] Cf. the expression *'tēn alētheian poien'*, 1 John 1[6], and the art. *'alētheia'* etc.
in *TWNT*, I, p. 233, by QUELL, KITTEL and BULTMANN.

*weak and you are strong. For your return to uprightness is all that we
ask.* (10) *That is why I am writing this to you being [still] absent from
you: it is so as not to have, when present with you, reason to cut you to
the quick by virtue of the power which the Lord has given me—for
building up and not for pulling down.* (11) *Meanwhile, my brothers, be*

direct it at the Corinthians, of course; but also to indicate the absence
of selfish preoccupations in true Apostles.

13⁹ sums up the developments of **13¹⁻⁸**: the Apostle would ask for
nothing better than to appear weak, and even to be weak, provided
that the Corinthians were truly strong, which will be the case if they
allow themselves to become upright again.[10] The allusion to those
who claimed to be strong (1 Cor 4¹⁰) is quite transparent.

13¹⁰ '*Apotomōs chrēzein*' = '*apotomia chrēzein*' = 'to use severity.'
But as these words are derived from the root '*temnō*' = 'to cut' the
B.d.Cent. rightly translates: 'cut to the quick.'—'*Kata tēn exousian*
. . .' = 'according to the power' which God has given me, goes
naturally with what follows; it is a question not of the power to use
severity, but of building up ('*eis oikodomēn*') and not of destroying
('*eis kathairesin*').

13¹¹ Closing exhortations and greetings. '*Katartizesthe*' (cf. v. 9) is
taken in the passive sense, 'let yourselves be set right,' by Allo and
Windisch, who refer to Hebrews 13²². But it could well be the middle
voice ('set yourselves right') or indeed the hithpaël type of reflexive
('set one another right'). The same problem applies to '*parakaleisthe*':
'be encouraged' or rather 'encourage one another,' as is suggested by
what follows, which insists on the relationships of the Corinthians
among themselves—they should live in harmony ('*to auto phroneite*')
and in peace ('*eirēneuete*'), then the God of love and peace will be with
them (a benediction in the form of a promise).[11] God will dwell
among men, if they abide in love. It is also very much the thought of
the First Epistle of John (cf. the well-known verse 4¹²). This does not
alter the fact that for Paul, as well as for 'John', in the final analysis,
God is the dispenser of love and of all good things; but He can with-
draw them from those who do not cultivate them.

[10] That is the true sense of '*katartisis*' = 'setting to rights,' given by Allo. The
B.d.Cent., as well as Osty, find here the idea of improvement. But the whole
passage seems to us to be dominated by the opposition of the fault and recovery
from it. The primitive sense of '*katartizō*' is moreover 'to restore to good condition'
(Plummer: 'setting right what has previously gone wrong'). The noun '*katartisis*'
is quite rare (in the Bible only at this piont). But the verb '*katartizō*' is common.
'*Katartismos*' occurs in Ephesians 4¹² and in Isaiah 38¹² in Symmachus' version
(according to the HATCH and REDPATH *Concordance*).

[11] Concerning v. 11b several unimportant variants are cited by Tischendorf
('*eirēnēs*' alone, or '*eirēnēs kai agapēs*').

joyful; set one another right, encourage one another, be of the same disposition. Live in peace, and the God of love and of peace will be with you. (12) *Greet one another with the Christian kiss. All Christians greet you.* (13) *May the grace of the Lord Jesus Christ and the love of God and the communion of the Holy Spirit be with you all!*

13[12] Concerning the Christian kiss (*'philēma hagion'*), cf. also 1 Corinthians 16[20] ; Romans 16[16]; 1 Thessalonians 5[26]; 1 Peter 5[14]; Acts 20[37]. Let us add that the Jews recognised the kiss as a sign of reconciliation.[12] This may explain the adoption, in Christian Churches, of this formality of doubtful desirability, which the 'Apostolic Constitutions' permitted only between man and man and woman and woman.[13] Among the apologists Athenagoras seems to have been particularly cautious (*Legatio pro Christianis* 32, *MPG* 6, col. 964); he quotes an apocryphal text, which claims that the kiss brings exclusion from eternal life, if it is accompanied by the slightest ulterior motive (*'eiper mikron tē dianoia paratholōtheiē'*).

13[13] the benediction in this verse has become, as is well known, an integral part of the majority of liturgies of the Christian Church. It is distinguished from the other Pauline benedictions by its clearly trinitarian form. The mention of Christ first can be explained by the great antiquity of the purely Christological formula used elsewhere (cf. 1 Corinthians 16[23]: 'may the grace of the Lord Jesus Christ be with you,' also 1 Thessalonians 5[28]; 2 Thessalonians 3[18]; Romans 16[20b]; similarly Galatians 6[18]; Philippians 4[23]).

The grace (*'charis'*) of Jesus Christ is a gift granted to all Christians, whatever their particular charisms may be, and merges with the gift of the Holy Spirit. Since the latter is mentioned again at the end, it may be thought that *'koinōnia tou pneumatos'* is not the sharing in the Spirit, but the 'communion' which it creates among believers,[14] as no doubt also in Philippians 2[1].

---

[12] On this subject the monograph by A. WÜNSCHE, *Der Kuss in Bibel, Talmud und Midrasch*, 1911, should be consulted. Unfortunately it was not accessible to us.

[13] II, 57, § 17 (ed Funk, 1905, p. 165) and VIII, 11, § 9 (Funk, p. 494). Cf. CABROL, *Dictionnaire d'archéologie chrétienne*, II, pp. 117ff. HASTINGS, *Dictionary of the Apostolic Church*, II, p. 443, thinks, with many others, that the primitive significance of the kiss was of a magical kind ('the forming of a covenant; for the soul flows out of the nose or the mouth').

[14] An interpretation extolled by Bachmann and by T. SCHMIDT, *Der Leib Christi*, 1914, p. 134f, also by DAVIES, p. 178.—Against: Lietzmann and HAUCK, *TWNT*, III, p. 807.—Furthermore, the wish to make explicit mention of the Holy Spirit must have been strengthened by the necessity of defending the originality of the Christian position in face of the disciples of the Baptist, who did not know or denied the Holy Spirit (cf. Acts 19[1–3]). Among the Mandaeans, who are to some extent Deutero-Baptists, the Holy Spirit is even considered as an evil power.

What this text does not prove is that the Spirit was personified.[15]
We are still a long way from the trinitarian doctrine of the Councils.

[15] As for the text of 3^{17}, which seems to identify the Spirit with the Lord, see our
remarks in this Commentary *ad loc.*—Furthermore, a different 'Trinity' from that
of Paul, namely 'Father, Mother, Son' may have developed in Judaeo-Christian
circles. At least the Gospel to the Hebrews speaks of the Holy Spirit as of the
mother of Jesus ('*ruaḥ*' is feminine). See the text preserved by ORIGEN, quoted
above *ad* 11^4; but this root has gone dry.—An ancient Jewish trinity, but of a
different type, is postulated by MORGENSTERN, *JBL*, 1945, p. 15f: El, Shaddai,
Eloah. On all questions about the '*pneuma*' in the Bible and in Hellenism, an
abundant bibliography can be found in *TWNT*, VI, pp. 330–3.

APPENDIX

REMARKS ON THE ORIGINS OF APOSTLESHIP ACCORDING TO THE NEW TESTAMENT.[1]

The Catholic conception of the essence and origin of the apostolate is almost entirely dominated by that of Mark, adopted on the one hand by 'Matthew', on the other by the writer of the Third Gospel and the Acts of the Apostles. In his conception, only the Twelve qualify for apostolic dignity. Logically applied, it can only make Paul subordinate to the Twelve. And that is why Acts, while praising his missionary work, avoids giving him the title of Apostle.[2] An effort is needed to escape from this one-sided view, against which the Apostle Paul continually protested, in order to have a clear picture of the ideas of early Christianity.

We shall return to Paul later. But let us first make it clear that even the account of the calling of the Twelve in Mark, the historical accuracy of which we do not wish to question, contains nothing exclusive, though it was doubtless thus interpreted by them. There is nothing to indicate that other Apostles are impossible in the future.[3]

Nor must it be forgotten that the Fourth Gospel gives far less importance to the rôle of the Twelve and provides no account of their call nor any list of the Twelve. In general it speaks of the disciples ('*mathētai*'), among whom are named in the first place the anonymous disciple (the 'beloved'), then Peter and some others, including Lazarus,[4] and Nathaniel, who was just as little one of the Twelve as the unknown disciple. The Gospel of Mark represents therefore only one of the possible ways of expounding the life of Jesus and His relationships with His disciples.

---

[1] Cf. *TWNT*, article '*apostolos*' and A. FRIDRICHSEN, *The Apostle and his Message*, in collection of works published by the University of Uppsala, fasc. 3, 1947.

[2] He is spoken of in this way twice only (14^4 and 14^{14}).

[3] In one sense the mission of the Seventy (Lk 9^{10}) confirms our view.

[4] May be identical to the 'beloved', cf. John 11^3; cf. FLOYD V. FILSON, 'Who was the beloved disciple?' *JBL*, 1949 pt 2.

As for the well-known prediction which announces the rôle as a rock for Cephas (Mt 16[18]),[5] we consider that this prophecy was fulfilled at the time of the setting up of the first Christian Church, which was the one in Jerusalem. It was indeed founded on Peter's preaching, according to Acts 2. But it goes without saying that this text (Mt 16) does not speak of the *direction* of the Church in Jerusalem (and still less of the one in Rome). One may be at the base of an edifice without being its coping.[6]

Returning to the question of apostleship, it is none the less curious that Paul also awards the title of Apostle to James, the brother of the Lord. Indeed, in the Epistle to the Galatians 1[18] he tells of his meeting with Peter in Jerusalem and adds: 'I saw none of the other Apostles except James, the brother of the Lord.'—In 1 Corinthians 15[6-7], where the appearances of Christ are under discussion, Paul says: 'He appeared to Cephas, then to the Twelve, then to five hundred Christians, and then to James, and then to all the Apostles.'[7] In Galatians 2[19] James is even mentioned first among the 'pillars' at Jerusalem. On what was the call of James based? Since there is absolutely no indication that he was converted in the lifetime of Jesus, it must be supposed that his apostleship was founded entirely on these appearances. The private appearance of Jesus to His brother is moreover expressly narrated in the Gospel to the Hebrews, a highly Judaeo-Christian writing, which naturally had an interest in emphasising it, but which we cannot, in view of Paul's text, accuse of having invented it.[8] The Twelve also seem to have made much of these appearances in addition to their call of which we have already spoken, in order not

---

[5] With O. CULLMANN, *Peter. Disciple-Apostle-Martyr*, ET London 1953, and H. CLAVIER, 'Petros kai Petra' in *Neutestamentliche Studien für R. Bultmann*, Berlin 1954, we admit the historicity of the prophecy which was, however, inserted in a very bad place. On this point see our *Royaume de Dieu selon Jésus et l'apôtre Paul*, 1938, pp. 111–27. Also the recent articles by E. Stauffer, who has very largely the same drift as ourselves in his exposition of this passage. See notably his study 'Messias oder Menschensohn?' in *New Testament Studies*, year 1, no. 2, pp. 81ff.

[6] The passage John 21[17] where Jesus says to Peter: 'Feed my lambs' could obviously be interpreted as a promise to entrust to him the direction of the Church. But apart from the fact that the narrative in John 21 must be interpreted in the light of the history of the early Church, it is significant that Mark, Matthew and Luke, who take so much trouble to speak highly of Peter's position, show no knowledge of it.

[7] Why is it not worded 'Once more to the Twelve' instead of 'To all the Apostles'? Without doubt because there were other Apostles besides James and the Twelve.

[8] Cf. JEROME, *De viris illustribus* 2 (text in LIETZMANN, *Kleine Texte* 3, p. 8.; translation in M. R. JAMES, *The Apocryphal New Testament*, Oxford 1924, p. 3f): 'Now the Lord, when he had given the linen cloth unto the servant of the priest, went unto James and appeared to him . . . Bring ye, saith the Lord, a table and bread, and . . . He took bread and blessed and brake and gave it unto James the Just and said unto him: My brother, eat thy bread, for the Son of Man is risen from among them that sleep.'

to lag behind. And we have a hint of these preoccupations in the text of Matthew 28^{18-19} in which the resurrected Lord confers on them an apostolic mission. If the call narrated in Mark 3^{11} had been judged sufficient, this account would have been much less necessary.
But there is more. It seems extremely probable to us that the rôle of James was not limited to an apostolic dignity which he shared with the Twelve. If one studies the Pauline texts carefully and distinguishes clearly the different strata of tradition in the Acts, the conviction grows that it was James who really directed the Church in Jerusalem. Let us return first to the account of the interview between Paul and Peter in Antioch according to Galatians 2^{11ff}. It not only reveals Paul's great independence with regard to Peter, but it certainly does not reveal Peter as head of the Church in Jerusalem. Peter behaves like a subordinate of James and defers before his envoys. The memory of these relationships has been preserved in the pseudo-Clementine writings, more precisely in the correspondence between Peter and James reproduced in this Judaeo-Christian literature. Even if these letters are complete forgeries, a point which is not absolutely proved, they seem to reflect an historical state of affairs, namely that James was the superior of Peter.[9]
But there are other indications on this subject. For anyone reading between the lines, it is clear that on the occasion of the Council of Jerusalem, reported in Acts 15^{1-29}, James is once again ranged among the Apostles. For an assembly of 'Apostles and Elders' is spoken of; now James has never been listed among the 'presbuteroi'. Then, and this is still more interesting, it is not Peter who presides over this assembly. He merely appears as advocate for Paul's case. It is James who directs the debates, and who proposes and formulates the resolution adopted by the assembly. It was certainly not the writer of Acts, a partisan of the concept of the Twelve Apostles, who invented such a rôle. Here we touch a bedrock layer of tradition which 'Luke' allows to show through almost in spite of himself.
The only question which can now arise is to ascertain whether this primacy of James dates only from the period when Paul had left Jerusalem, as O. Cullmann claims.[10] Eusebius, relying on Clement of Alexandria, relates a tradition according to which James was chosen *from the beginning* as 'bishop' of Jerusalem (*Hist.Eccl.* II, Ch. 1, § 3). This information seems interesting, putting aside the

---

[9] In the 'Preachings of Peter' (the important part of this writing), Peter appears to be obliged to give him an account of his missionary activity: 'Every doctor and every apostle should have the warrant of his authority' (O. CULLMANN, *Le problème littéraire et historique du roman pseudo-clémentin, EHPR*, 23, pp. 250ff).
—On the rôle attributed to Peter in the other parts of the pseudo-Clementine romance, see also H. CLAVIER, 'La primauté de Pierre d'après les Pseudo-Clémentines,' *RHPR*, 1956, pp. 298–307. According to H.Ch. PUECH and G. QUISPEL (*Vigiliae Christianae*, vol. 8, pts. 1–2) the famous Jung Codex contains a 'letter of James,' in which the latter also appears as superior to the Twelve.
[10] O. CULLMANN, *Peter*, ET 41f.

anachronistic title of bishop. In any case we think that we can reach a more coherent conception of events by recognising that, immediately after the resurrection of Jesus, James to some extent became His successor, and that the Eleven or the Twelve grouped themselves around him, as they had formerly done around Jesus. It is the beginning of a 'caliphate', a view admirably developed by Johannes Weiss.[11] This is rooted in the Messianic concept of the Jerusalem Church, which had to be and wished to be directed by descendants of David. That is why after the martyrdom of James, the direction of the Church was entrusted to Simeon, a cousin of Jesus; then, after the exodus of the community to Pella, to Jude, another brother of Jesus, and then to his descendants. Even Domitian was for a time worried by the ascendancy which the 'Messiahs' of this dynasty had achieved.[12] If in the long run this 'caliphate' did not achieve greater importance, this fact is largely due to the destruction of Jerusalem,[13] which turned the Transjordanian Judaeo-Christians into a sect without great importance for the main body of the Christian Church.

In any case we gather that Paul on one side, and the Twelve on the other, had trouble in establishing their position, in view of the way events turned soon after the death and resurrection of Jesus, and we shall give full credit to the enlightening article of M. Goguel who ascribes the 'Tu es Petrus' of Matthew 16 to the controversies which took place on this subject.[14] We gather now that Paul must have had to struggle to some extent on two fronts, on one side against the pretended exclusive privilege of the Twelve which acquired concrete form in the somewhat Petrine Gospel of Mark—on the other hand against the pretensions of James and his brothers to direct the Churches. The Apostle Paul never conceded that his apostleship dated from something like an investiture by the Twelve or by James. His status dates from the direct call received from the Lord on the Damascus

---

[11] J. WEISS, *The History of Primitive Christianity*, London 1937, pp. 369ff. According to this penetrating historian, who naturally relies on Hegesippus, the election of Simeon after the martyrdom of James shows that belonging to the messianic household of David was what mattered, even if one was not the brother of Jesus. We think that this idea dates from the earliest period of the Church. This also seems to be the opinion of H. CLAVIER, *RHPR*, 1956, p. 304.

[12] It is hardly necessary to stress that the Messianic concept among the Jews can very easily be accommodated to the idea of a dynasty of Messiahs of Davidic origin. This is in all probability the most ancient conception; see the conclusive texts studied in our *Royaume de Dieu*, pp. 57ff. The texts of Hegesippus have been preserved for us by EUSEBIUS, *Hist.Eccl.*, Bk IV, especially Chs 8, 11, 19, 20, 21.

[13] On this point see S. G. F. BRANDON, *The Fall of Jerusalem and the Christian Church*, London 1951.

[14] M. GOGUEL, 'Tu es Petrus,' *Bulletin de la Faculté libre de théologie protestante de Paris*, 1938; also *The Birth of Christianity*, ET London 1953, pp. 113ff.

road.[15] But he goes still further; God the Father Himself chose him before he was born (Gal 1[15]), like Jeremiah (Jer 1[5]), something which none of the other Apostles ever claimed. In the light of this passage, expressions like 'through God the Father' (*'dia theou patros,'* Gal 1[1]) or 'through the will of God' (*'dia thelēmatos theou,'* 1 Cor 1[1], 1[1]) show up as something much more serious than a simple manner of speaking, or an allusion to the general control of events by God.

But here we must tackle another question. Everything makes us believe that the Jerusalem Apostles and especially James claimed the right if not to have full direction, at least to have oversight of all the Christian Churches. Witness the mission of Peter and John to Samaria (Acts 8[14-25]); they were undoubtedly sent by James, although 'Luke' naturally does not say so. They were to coordinate the Christian movement which had been set in motion there by the preaching of Philip the Evangelist. They oppose Simon Magus, who, however, according to the preceding narrative (Acts 8[13]) had already been baptised. They wished, at that early stage, *'kataskopēsai'* = 'to inspect,' as Paul will say in Galatians 2[4]. Witness also and especially the counter-propaganda of the Judaeo-Christian missionaries in Galatia; and if we cannot prove that all the 'false apostles' against whom Paul battled were envoys from Jerusalem, we can however accept this of those among them who claimed to be 'arch-apostles'. We even know that the brothers of Jesus did some missionary work themselves (1 Cor 9[5]); although we know nothing about Churches founded by them, they evidently tried in the course of their journeys to leave their mark in the Churches founded by Paul, Barnabas or others.

Perhaps Paul would have reacted less violently against the pretensions of Jerusalem to hegemony if its emissaries had not sometimes preached 'another Gospel,' that is primarily the obligation imposed on the Gentiles to adhere to the commandments of the Law, and that in spite of the quite liberal decision reported in Acts 15 (cf. 9–10), the full scope of which Luke may not have understood.[16] In any case, the doctrinal division made any ecclesiastical subordination impossible—

---

[15] It would be necessary to be able to cite here extracts from almost all the Pauline Epistles. Let us remember 'Paul, an apostle, not from men, neither through man, but through Jesus Christ, and God the Father,' Galatians 1[1]. It seems clear to us that Paul's vision on the Damascus road was sufficient in his eyes to ensure the status and authenticity of his apostleship. If he nevertheless tries to put that vision on the same level as the appearances of the Risen Lord on earth in Judaea (and in Galilee? cf. 1 Cor 15[8]), it was assuredly to check a conception of apostleship which excluded those who had not had appearances of the same type.

[16] We cannot study here the much-debated question of the date and scope of the celebrated decrees of the 'Council' of Jerusalem, nor of its relation with the meeting reported by the Epistle to the Galatians. We refer the reader therefore to the important work of E. TROCMÉ, *Le 'Livre des Actes' et l'Histoire,* Paris, 1957.

even if any question of apostolic authority were set aside. Yet the Apostle Paul by making himself responsible for the collection in pagan lands on behalf of the 'saints' in Jerusalem, nevertheless recognised certain obligations in respect of the mother-Church. There are perhaps grounds for thinking that this collection was destined to take the place of the tribute sent by the Diaspora to the Temple, and was thus a way of showing respect to the dignity of the Holy City.

In conclusion, we find then in early Christianity several conceptions of apostleship. (1) The apostleship reserved for the Twelve called by Jesus in His lifetime (those who knew Christ in the flesh, as Paul says in 5[16]). (2) Apostleship in a wider sense based on an appearance of the Lord after His resurrection in Judaea. In this sense James and others could be called Apostles. Paul rejects the first conception and accepts the second, applying it to himself. (3) However, in the case of the Apostle Paul we can surmise still another and very personal conception of his apostleship. He was called according to a decree of God, by the heavenly vision on the Damascus road, which was evidently of a different kind from the appearances of Jesus on earth, even though the Apostle, for reasons of apologetics, strives to bring it into line with the other appearances. (4) There must have existed a Messianic conception of something like a special apostleship reserved for the members of the family of Jesus, the family being considered as having King David as ancestor.

If we have insisted more on the differences between the notions of apostleship than on their unity, which is indisputable, it is to assist in understanding the position of the Apostle Paul.

We recognise also that we have not yet been able to resolve all the problems. What was the precise basis of the apostleship of Barnabas and Apollos, who are expressly called 'apostoloi' by Paul (1 Cor 4[9]; 9[6]).[17]—Must we apply to them the rather more worldly Jewish conception of apostleship (an ambassador of a Church) or must we postulate still another notion of apostleship in which certain charismata manifesting the power of the Spirit were considered as sufficient testimony of the authenticity of apostolic status (cf. 1 Cor 12[28] and 12[12])? Moreover, a complete study of the question, which we have not been able to undertake here, would have to explain the exact sense and the origin of the apostolate which is presupposed in the *Didache*.

Note

To return to the Eleven and the Twelve, we are of the opinion that the historical accuracy of the well-known command given in Mat-

---

[17] We omit Andronicus and Junius, because the text of Romans 16[7], '*hoitines episēmoi en tois apostolois*,' could simply mean 'of repute among the Apostles.'

thew 28^{19} to go into all lands to teach and to baptise Gentiles is very doubtful. In fact the Twelve, apart from Peter, seem to have done very little missionary work. We are therefore led to agree with J. Weiss who explains that this description of the functions of the Twelve Apostles (according to Matthew 28^{19}; Luke 24^{47}; Acts 1^{8}) is the later ecclesiastical conception, which is here taken back to the beginning (*The History of Primitive Christianity*, ET, vol. I, p. 46; vol. II, p. 661).